From MASON To MINISTER

Through the Lattice

Praise for *From Mason to Minister – Through the Lattice*

From Mason to Minister – Through the Lattice is a captivating journey of courage through a world of secrets, soul-searching, and ultimate success. An intriguing and inspiring read from shadows to sunlight!

William J. Federer

Best-selling author, nationally known speaker, and presenter of *American Minute* on radio and Internet at AmericanMinute.com
President, Amerisearch Inc., St. Louis, Missouri

Neil is an accomplished writer and poet and his gifts show up loud and clear in this autobiographical book of his journey through Freemasonry toward the solid rock of Calvinism. Having come there myself along a very different road, it truly amazes me to learn how God leads His elect in various ways back to the great Jehovah Elohim without Whom no one can come to God. I heartily recommend this readable book.

Rev. Professor Emeritus Dr. Francis Nigel Lee

Queensland Presbyterian Theological College
Brisbane, Queensland, Australia

By its very nature, Freemasonry is shrouded in mystery and cloaked in secrecy, which has led inevitably to much misunderstanding and misinformation. It is here Brother McKinlay's book comes to the rescue. Neither an apologetic nor a polemic, it is the memoir of his conversion to Christ after his personal membership in Freemasonry, how he moved *From Mason to Minister*. His journey, seen *Through the Lattice* (Song of Solomon 2), is charming, engaging, informative, historical, and, most of all, Biblical. It is unique – as is typical of Nordskog Publishing – and answers some questions about a controversial subject. It is a book to be enjoyed.

Dr. J. D. Watson

Pastor-Teacher, Grace Bible Church, Meeker, Colorado
Author of *A Word for the Day* and *A Hebrew Word for the Day*

I read a lot of books. Many different kinds. Some just for entertainment. The ones I look out for most keenly, however, those that I seek like pearls without price, are books like this. Books that get me in touch with God. As a Christian (though not a Calvinist) I consider this to be treasure. Especially so given that I know the person whose experiences are related. There is a sense (it seems to me) that only literature of this kind is actually important.

Billy Scobie

aka Alexander Tait, Author of *Whisky in the Jar* and *The Cup*,
and the upcoming novel *Upon This Rock*
Alexandria, Dunbartonshire, Scotland

From M⊕SON To MINISTER

Through the Lattice

Neil Cullan McKinlay

Nordskog Publishing inc.

Ventura, California

2011

From Mason to Minister
Through the Lattice
by Neil Cullan McKinlay

Copyright © 2011 by Neil Cullan McKinlay

International Standard Book Number: 978-0-9827074-7-0
Library of Congress Control Number: 2011920376

Theology Editor: Ronald W. Kirk
Manuscript Editor: Kimberley Winters Woods
Managing Editor and Book Design: Desta Garrett

Cover Painting: *Airless Spaceman*, by Fearghas MacFhionnlaigh,
the author's brother, who also inspired the cover design.
Cover Photo: *Ocean Sunrise*, by Ken's Photos–Ken Sjodin

Printed in the United States of America

Published by

Nordskog Publishing Inc.

Nordskog Publishing, Inc.
2716 Sailor Avenue
Ventura, California 93001, USA
1-805-642-2070 • 1-805-276-5129
www.NordskogPublishing.com

Member
spa
Christian Small Publishers Association

Dedication

To my father and my mother,

Stuart McKinlay and Catherine McKinlay (nee Nugent),

with grateful thanks to the Triune God.

About the Author

NEIL CULLAN MCKINLAY was ordained as a minister of the Presbyterian Church of Australia in 1998. He became an Australian Army Chaplain in 2008.

He is married to Dorothy, and they have three grown up daughters: Jennifer, Nina, and Fionna.

Neil is Canadian born, but was raised in Scotland. Dorothy and he migrated to Canada from Scotland in 1980 and began a family. They moved to Australia's sunny shores with their three daughters in 1990 and have resided there ever since.

Neil writes for a monthly Australian writer's magazine called *FreeXpresSion*. He self-published a collection of these writings in a book titled *The Song of Creation and Other Contemplations* (ISBN 0-9757588-7-X).

His big brother Fearghas MacFhionnlaigh is a constant encouragement to his faith and was instrumental in the writing of *From Mason to Minister*.

Author's Preface

THERE are many books, tracts, and pamphlets that have been written by Christians that seek to illustrate the incompatibility of Christianity with Freemasonry. Indeed there have been books and articles written by Christians who are Freemasons attempting to demonstrate the opposite! Though I am a Christian, this book is not an attempt to sway the reader either way. I simply wish to tell the story of how I, by the grace of God, was converted to Christianity after joining, and then regularly attending, Masonic lodges in Manitoba, Canada.

Are the pillars of Masonic morality the same as those that undergird Christianity? Again, the purpose of my book is not to spell out the answer to this. Therefore, rather than attempt to answer that question here, I'll simply let you, the reader, make up your own mind. I hope you will be pleased to come on a journey with me as I recall events in my life, some of which were life-transforming. I'll engage you in a little history, adventure, geography, theology, some humour, and philosophical musings. Sure, you might not always agree with everything I say, but that doesn't mean we can't still be friends on the journey. All I ask is that you come with me. I'll try to anticipate questions and comments you might like to make, but you will have to pardon me if I do all the talking!

It's not my intention to expose Freemasonry to criticism, ridicule, or scorn. There are exposés aplenty dating back hundreds of years. There is no need for another! However, for the purpose of relating my story I will need to mention in a general way something of the lodge workings. Please forgive me if you think I've gone too far. A quote from a book, that helped me early on to understand the inner workings of Freemasonry (in Canada) should suffice to allay any fears Freemasons may have that my book is yet another in the long list of Masonic exposés. I apply the following quote to what I also have written:

> Does the writing of a book such as this violate the obligation of secrecy? No. Freemasonry is not a secret society; it is a society with secrets. The secrets which a Mason pledges himself never to write or to see written consist of certain of the ceremonies and modes of recognition. They do not include Masonic truths, which are accessible to all. They may be found in the VOSL [Volume of the Sacred Law, i.e., the Bible], but their discovery and their interpretation are left to each man. The prime object of Masonry is to assist our brethren in discovering these tenets and principles.
> (*Beyond the Pillars*, Grand Lodge of A.F. and A.M.
> of Canada in the Province of Ontario, 1973, 99)

I am a Christian, a Calvinist, Reformed in my theology, and an ordained minister in the Presbyterian Church of Australia. My story begins in Scotland, moves to Canada, and finishes in Australia. I didn't plan it that way – I'm not that good at planning things – it's just the way it happened in the Providence of God. For the record, I cut my ties with Freemasonry in 1990 when, with my young family, I left Canada for Australia.

Contents

CONTENTS

Introduction

A MASON is one who builds edifices of stone. A minister is one who edifies or builds up people. Freemasonry is that which seeks to build up its members by using analogies from the building (and the destruction and rebuilding) of Solomon's Temple. Solomon's Temple was a magnificent work of art. The specifics for the construction of the Temple were given by revelation of God. Though perfectly functional, everything to do with the Temple symbolized something greater. King Solomon himself is a type; Jesus Christ is the greater. Christ is the anti-type. It is to Him that the Temple and everything in it pointed. And every animal sacrifice made at the Temple pointed to the Ultimate Sacrifice.

Solomon's father, King David, the sweet psalmist of Israel, was a man of war. Solomon was a man of peace. The glory and splendour of his kingdom was not just the magnificent Temple in the great City of Jerusalem. Rather Solomon's reign was a time of peace like there had never been on earth since mankind rebelled against God in Adam in the Garden of Eden. This peace typified the peace that God had promised the Prince of Peace Himself would bring.

Before Solomon started building the Temple, God invited him to ask of Him anything he wanted:

> Now the king went to Gibeon to sacrifice there, for that was the great high place: Solomon offered a thousand burnt offerings on that altar. At Gibeon the LORD appeared to Solomon in a dream by night; and God said, "Ask! What shall I give you?" And Solomon said: "You have shown great mercy to Your servant David my father, because he walked before You in truth, in righteousness, and in uprightness of heart with You; You have continued this great kindness for him, and You have given him a son to sit on his throne, as it is this day. Now, O LORD my God, You have made Your servant king instead of my father David, but I am a little child; I do not know how to go out or come in. And Your servant is in the midst of Your people whom You have chosen, a great people, too numerous to be numbered or counted. Therefore give to Your servant an understanding heart to judge Your people, that I may discern between good and evil. For who is able to judge this great people of Yours? (1 Kings 3:4–9)

The LORD God granted Solomon's petition and also promised him things he didn't request; things such as riches and honor. But even the wisdom God granted Solomon was a *type* of one greater than Solomon: Jesus Christ, who is Wisdom incarnate.

> And God gave Solomon wisdom and exceedingly great understanding, and largeness of heart like the sand on the seashore. Thus Solomon's wisdom excelled the wisdom of all the men of the East and all the wisdom of Egypt. For he was wiser than all men – than Ethan the Ezrahite, and Heman, Chalcol, and Darda, the sons of Mahol; and his fame was in the surrounding nations. He spoke three thousand proverbs, and his songs were one thousand and five. Also he spoke of trees, from the cedar tree of Lebanon even to the hyssop that springs out of the wall; he spoke also of animals, of birds, of creeping things, and of fish. And men of all nations, from all the kings of the earth who had heard of his wisdom, came to hear the wisdom of Solomon. (1 Kings 4:29–34)

As a lost sinner, dead in my trespasses and my sins, as a leafless tree on the frozen wasteland of a severe winter, I asked, nay, I begged God to let me know Him, to let me have a deep and intimate relationship with Him. He replied by giving me His only begotten Son, Jesus Christ.

> The voice of my beloved!
> Behold, he comes
> Leaping upon the mountains,
> Skipping upon the hills.
> My beloved is like a gazelle
>   or a young stag.
> Behold, he stands behind our wall;
> He is looking through the windows,
> Gazing through the lattice.
> My beloved spoke, and said to me:
> "Rise up, my love, my fair one,
> And come away.
> For lo, the winter is past,
> The rain is over and gone.
> The flowers appear on the earth;
> The time of singing has come,
> And the voice of the turtle dove
> Is heard in our land.
> The fig tree puts forth her green figs,
> And the vines with the tender grapes
> Give a good smell.
> Rise up, my love, my fair one,
> And come away!
> O my dove, in the clefts of the rock,
> In the secret places of the cliff,
> Let me see your face,
> Let me hear your voice;
> For your voice is sweet,
> And your face is lovely."
>
> – Song of Solomon 2:8–14

PART
ONE

Pre-Masonry

Geographical, Philosophical, and Religious Background

*F*OR me, growing up in Scotland meant varying amounts of exposure to Christianity and its teachings. That's just the way it was. At home we never had any of those plaques on the wall saying that Jesus was the head of our house or anything like that. In fact, I can't say I heard anything of Jesus Christ in my home when I was growing up.

My father was a communist who worked in the shipyards on the Red Clydeside. He would often recite poetry from memory – even in the course of conversation. My mother taught me to love nature. She had a beautiful singing voice that brought comfort to her five children. My parents instilled in me a deep appreciation of Scottish flora and fauna, and taught me the art of contemplation.

My mother would feed the blackbirds pieces of cheese as they came to the kitchen window for handouts. One of her favourite birds was the little robin who would appear from his travels at a certain time each year. She seemed to have some sort of mystical rapport with the birds. A red-breasted robin entered through her bedroom window and perched on the foot of her bed the day she died. I penned the following while living in Canada:

> Blackbird's on the telegraph pole,
> Singing songs of love,
> Songs that elevate the soul,
> Tunes from up above,
> My mother's in the kitchen cooking,
> Singing harmony,
> The music drifts across the miles to me.

Though they were from Scotland, my mum and dad spent most of the 1950s in Ontario, Canada, where I was born. They returned to Scotland with my two older brothers and me when I was two or three. I know that my mum and dad weren't hostile to the idea of the various public schools I attended in the Vale of Leven herding me, along with the rest of the pupils, to church at Christmas and Easter. And I'm pleased to add that, in God's good time, both my parents also eventually came to embrace Christ and His claims.

Since all Protestant or public schools in our area were attached to a church (e.g., the Church of Scotland), it was inevitable that one of their ministers would visit the school. I remember one minister awarding sweets to any pupil who could recite from memory the Apostles' Creed.* I don't remember receiving any sweets, but I did commit the Creed to memory.

For a few months when I was in my late teens, I attended the Jamestown Parish church with my schoolmate, Jim. The timing of the service was very handy as its closing coincided with the opening of the Rowan Tree Bar on the opposite side of the street. Ordinarily, we were happier when we left the pub than when we left the church!

The only conscious memory I have of anything the preacher talked about in his Sunday morning sermons was related to pubs. One Sunday, he talked about an astronaut who was back on earth telling some of his mates about the time he had landed on the moon. "What was it like?" the astronaut's friends inquired. "Well," said the astronaut, "There is a pub on the moon." "A pub?" they repeated. "Yes, a pub," he replied. "And what is this pub like?" asked his mates. To which the astronaut replied, "It isn't very good. It has no atmosphere!"

I wonder, did the "Happy Padre" mention this to get my attention and Jim's?

I suppose when all these things are added together, along with the few years I spent in the Boys' Brigade,** it could be assumed that my young life had been shot through with a wide-spread buckshot of Christianity. These "holes" let in light. Back then, Christianity would rattle around in one of my brain-hemispheres, like the ball bearing

---

* See Apostles' Creed in Glossary, p. 185.

** The Boys' Brigade (which had a junior section called the Life Boys) was founded in Glasgow in 1883 by William Alexander Smith for "The advancement of Christ's Kingdom among Boys and the promotion of habits of Reverence, Discipline, Self-Respect, and all that tends towards a true Christian Manliness."

in a shaken can of spray-paint, whilst the other hemisphere had the moss-covered rolling stone of evolution bumping around in it – an epistemological "brain imbalance" if there ever was one!

I suppose like everyone else who has been taught two competing worldviews, I tried to leap the synapse gaps by having faith that the "missing link" would eventually be found. So, at the time, I thought that not only had God created a revolving world, He must also have made it an evolving world.

I received a smattering of Christianity by attending the Boys' Brigade first in Alexandria, but then I joined the Jamestown Boys' Brigade where I had attended Life Boys some years before. Some of the words of the song we sang quite a lot when in the Boys' Brigade stuck with me:

> Will your anchor hold in the storms of life,
> When the clouds unfold their wings of strife?
> When the strong tides lift, and the cables strain,
> Will your anchor drift, or firm remain?
> We have an anchor that keeps the soul
> Steadfast and sure while the billows roll;
> Fastened to the Rock which cannot move,
> Grounded firm and deep in the Saviour's love!
>
> – Priscilla Jane Owens (1829–1907)

What was my anchor? Back then, I was at sea. And now I believe a person only really discovers what his or her anchor is when he or she goes through the storms of life. I was a young man with a "tension headache" created by two conflicting worldviews, about to "set sail" into the sunset.

When I was a young man, I thought I was a Christian. I didn't know I wasn't until, by the grace of God, I became one!

Gateway to the World

$\mathcal{M}$Y later teen years brought with them a fascination with the idea of Freemasonry. I asked my dad if he was one, and was saddened to hear that he wasn't. He said he didn't need Freemasonry to get through life. You could become a lodge-member at age eighteen provided your dad was. But I would have to wait till I was twenty-one. I had put in an application when my twenty-first birthday loomed like the sun beginning to rise in the east, but before my lodge-application could be blackballed it was overshadowed by my planned departure for Canada.

"Go west, young man!" was a refrain that was constantly per-ambulating in my mind. A Christian even came out with a song with the refrain, "Go west, young man – and let sin go east." Was I subconsciously attempting to flee my sins in Scotland by moving west to Canada? If so, is it possible for a person to escape the pres-ence of God?

> Take I the morning wings, and dwell
> in utmost parts of sea;
> Ev'n there, Lord, shall Thy hand me lead,
> Thy right hand hold shall me.
> If I do say that darkness shall
> me cover from Thy sight,
> Then surely shall the very night
> about me be as light.
> Yea, darkness hideth not from Thee,
> but night doth shine as day:
> To Thee the darkness and the light
> are both alike alway.
>
> The Church of Scotland's
> Revised Church Hymnary (RCH)
> – Psalm 139:9–12

A Sense of Adventure

*A*s a precursor to joining the lodge, a couple of mates and myself invented a "secret order." It involved a series of hand-signals and gestures that would make a baseball catcher jealous. Mind you, to the uninitiated, we must have looked like we all had a bad case of body and head lice. Our meeting hall was mostly the pub, hence our name: Bent Elbow Squad (BES). I've forgotten what the penalty was for disclosing BES secrets – I probably owe a round of drinks to my mates!

BES lost one of its founding members when I returned to Canada in September 1977, just in time to celebrate my twenty-first birthday; which I didn't, at least not the way we would have celebrated it in Scotland! There we would probably have had a good night at the Loch Lomond Amateur Rowing Club at Balloch, a town that some call the Gateway to the Highlands.

Back then, the clubhouse was an excellent facilitator of a great social evening. There we had spent many a Saturday evening celebrating our regatta wins or drowning our losses. More healthfully, it was a relief after a hard row to douse the flames of lungs on fire by simply scooping-up peat-flavoured water straight from Loch Lomond in our blistered hands. The water was soft to the touch and provided cool, velvety relief to our parched throats.

It was a life worth lapping up. But the "call of the wild" had to be answered.

There seems to be an insatiable thirst for knowledge inherent in man from the very moment of his birth. But do any of us ever really outgrow the "what's that?" phase of life? I'm sure this must be what is being spoken of in the Scripture that states, "And He has made from one blood every nation of men to dwell on all the face of the earth, and has determined their pre-appointed times and the boundaries of their dwellings, so that they should seek the Lord, in the hope that they might grope for Him and find Him, though He is not far from each of us" (Acts 17:26–27).

Could it be, then, that our thirst for knowledge and our sense of adventure is our God-given desire to seek and to grope for the One the Bible calls the Creator and Redeemer of this world? The gravitational pull of the moon causes the tide to ebb and flow twice every twenty-four hours. Would God draw me to Himself – or would He repel me?

> Holy, holy, holy, Lord God Almighty!
> All Thy works shall praise Thy Name
> In earth and sky and sea;
> Holy, holy, holy, merciful and mighty,
> God in Three Persons, blessed Trinity!
>
> — Reginald Heber (1783–1826)
> Hymn 1, RCH

Solomonic Insight

Tales of Utopia might be the title of the recurrent dream in everyman's mind, including mine! Could it be that Utopia is simply a genetic memory etched in the psyche of man? Are we remembering, perhaps, the Garden of Eden before the Fall? Is our collective yearning for a better world caused by splinters from the trees of that perfect place, splinters of wood deeply embedded in our conscience?

All religions have their utopias. The Buddhist has his nirvana. The Muslim has his virgins in the afterlife and calls it heaven; the Jew his perfect political state; the Marxist his workers' utopia. But upon what pattern are these utopias modelled? Is there a utopian "blueprint"? The Christian model is the Garden of Eden – Paradise prepared for mankind by God. However, it is not simply a return to that perfect place. Rather, it is the raw materials found in Eden built into a permanent dwelling. This is what the Bible refers to as Heaven. Jesus will unite Heaven and the renewed Earth when He returns bodily with all His heavenly entourage.

Heaven for the Christian includes, in a manner of speaking, trees from Eden sawn into planks, planed, and adorned with gold, built into a habitation for God in His people. The completed Temple at Jerusalem built by King Solomon best illustrates the Biblical Heaven. The cooperation involved between the workers is itself an illustration of mankind in the Garden before the Fall, and mankind's return to the Garden, i.e., Heaven. To illustrate:

> Then Solomon sent to Hiram king of Tyre, saying: As you have dealt with David my father, and sent him cedars to build himself a house to dwell in, so deal with me. Behold, I am building a temple for the name of the LORD my God, to dedicate it to Him, to burn before Him sweet incense, for the continual showbread, for the burnt offerings morning and evening, on the Sabbaths, on the New Moons, and on the set feasts of the LORD our God. This is an ordinance forever to Israel.
>
> And the temple which I build will be great, for our God is greater than all gods. But who is able to build Him a temple, since heaven and the heaven of heavens cannot contain Him? Who am I then, that I should build Him a temple, except to burn sacrifice before Him?
>
> Therefore send me at once a man skillful to work in gold and silver, in bronze and iron, in purple and crimson and blue, who has skill to engrave with the skillful men who are with me in Judah and Jerusalem, whom David my father provided. Also send me cedar and cypress and algum logs from Lebanon, for I know that your servants have skill to cut timber in Lebanon; and indeed my servants will be with your servants, to prepare timber for me in abundance, for the temple which I am about to build shall be great and wonderful.
>
> And indeed I will give to your servants, the woodsmen who cut timber, twenty thousand kors of ground wheat, twenty thousand kors of barley, twenty thousand baths of wine, and twenty thousand baths of oil. (2 Chronicles 2:3–10)

Hiram, king of Tyre, was only too happy to oblige and also sent to Solomon his master craftsman, a man named Hiram, who was "skilled to work in gold and silver, bronze and iron, stone and wood, purple and blue, fine linen and crimson, and to make any engraving and to accomplish any plan which may be given to him" (2 Chron. 2:14). Masonic lore, as I was to learn, makes much of Hiram the master craftsman (sometimes referred to as Huram). "He was the son of a widow from the tribe of Naphtali, and his father was a man of Tyre, a bronze worker; he was filled with wisdom and understanding and skill in working with all kinds of bronze work. So he came to King Solomon and did all his work" (1 Kings 7:14).

Reminiscent of the peace and harmony in the Garden of Eden (and as a reflection of the Triune God), these three men – King Solomon, Hiram king of Tyre, and Hiram the master craftsman – worked together as one. Indeed, inside the temple there were plenty of reminders of the Garden of Eden from the wood panelling to the carved palm trees, flowers, pomegranates, and cherubim, etc. "The inside of the temple was cedar, carved with ornamental buds and open flowers. All was cedar; there was no stone to be seen" (1 Kings 6:18).

Solomon's Temple was stone on the outside and wood on the inside, which is like Paradise, the Garden of Eden. For in the Bible the word "paradise" (in Old Testament Hebrew) means a forest, park, or orchard, and its New Testament counterpart means the same thing, but the Koine Greek word itself is made up of two words meaning "a wall around." Thus the Garden of Eden is a walled park or orchard containing assorted trees, flora, and fauna. Therefore, in its fully matured and completed state, Heaven to the Christian is a real and physical place, with real and physical plants, trees, birds and animals. However, Paradise is the original Garden of Eden fully developed by the Spirit of Christ as the "last Adam," as per the "Cultural Mandate," as seen in this passage:

> Then God said, "Let Us make man in Our image, according to Our likeness; let them have dominion over the fish of the sea, over the birds of the air, and over the cattle, over all the earth and over every creeping thing that creeps on the

earth." So God created man in His own image; in the image of God He created him; male and female He created them. Then God blessed them, and God said to them, "Be fruitful and multiply; fill the earth and subdue it; have dominion over the fish of the sea, over the birds of the air, and over every living thing that moves on the earth." (Genesis 1:26–28)

Noah building the ark and Solomon building the Temple are two prime examples of what I mean by being obedient to the Cultural Mandate. In these, the micro symbolises the macro! Being humanity's federal head and representative, Adam (along with his posterity in him) failed to uphold the Cultural Mandate by eating the forbidden fruit. However, Jesus, as the new Adam (and the federal head and representative of His people) does not fail to keep the Cultural Mandate. Even now He is fulfilling it through His obedient posterity, i.e., the adopted children of God. For He says, "Do not think that I came to destroy the Law or the Prophets. I did not come to destroy but to fulfill. For assuredly, I say to you, till heaven and earth pass away, one jot or one tittle will by no means pass from the law till all is fulfilled" (Matt. 5:17–18). And, as the Apostle Paul says under inspiration of the Holy Spirit, "For we are His workmanship, created in Christ Jesus for good works, which God prepared beforehand that we should walk in them" (Eph. 2:10). Therefore, regenerated by the Spirit of Jesus Christ (the new Adam), believers are to do everything "to the glory of God" (1 Cor. 10:31). Individually and collectively, they are to build their culture on Jesus Christ. "For no other foundation can anyone lay than that which is laid, which is Jesus Christ. Now if anyone builds on this foundation with gold, silver, precious stones, wood, hay, straw, each one's work will become clear; for the Day will declare it, because it will be revealed by fire; and the fire will test each one's work, of what sort it is" (1 Cor. 3:11–13). Thus I believe that the new Adam is presently, by His Spirit indwelling believers, doing exactly what the first Adam (and mankind in him) was commissioned to do, i.e., keep and fulfill the Cultural Mandate. The Cultural Mandate, then, may be completed before Christ returns, "…for the earth shall be full of the knowledge [of the glory] of the LORD as the waters cover the sea" (Isa. 11:9b, cf. Hab. 2:14).

An Expanding Life and Worldview

*M*Y world expanded with my arrival on the Canadian Shield.* It was easy to meet on the level and part on the square in the vast flatness of southern Ontario. The Old World became the new as I knelt on the shores of Lake Huron's Georgian Bay at Penetanguishene. I didn't know God personally, but I sensed something of His awesomeness as I looked out across the bay, straining to see its other side. I tasted its water expecting salty bitterness but, instead, a fresh excitement washed over me.

I had gone to the "cottage at the lake" soon after my arrival in Canada. The couple that took me into their care was originally from Glasgow, and their son-in-law was from Newfoundland, a "Newfy." He would stroll the strand of one of the Great Lakes looking for driftwood. Then he'd turn his findings into beautiful coffee tables and the like. I've tried to sum up my impression of him with the following prose:

> Walking on a lonely beach
> To see what I might find
> It may not seem like much to you
> This quiet peace of mind
> The waves deliver to the shore
> A treasure of debris

---

* The Canadian Shield — also called the Laurentian Plateau, or Bouclier canadien (French) — is a massive geological shield covered by a thin layer of soil that forms the nucleus of the North American or Laurentia craton. It is an area mainly covered by igneous rock, which relates to its long volcanic history. It has a deep, common, joined bedrock region in eastern and central Canada and stretches north from the Great Lakes to the Arctic Ocean, covering over half of Canada. It also extends south into the northern reaches of the United States. Source: Wikipedia.

And pile the driftwood on the sand
   Some ship that died at sea?
   – long ago.
I bundle up the bits of lumber
   And branches from an old tree
I'll take them home to lacquer and paint
   And I'll sell them for a fee
For the marketplace is full of people
   Who think they're pretty smart
But in my heart I think they're crazy
   For they're buying my works of art!
   – pay the price.
I guess at times I've wondered
   What life is all about
I know I'll make it on my own
   No one need help me out
But I dream of home where fishing boats
   Are sailing out to sea
And at times I wish I'd never left the Bay
   For the Great Lakes can never be
   – the sea to me.

I knew how my friend from the East felt. But, like a Prairie sod-buster, rain, snow or shine, he was determined to make it in our "new-found land." And so was I.

Going Round in Circles

THE Masonic lodge had to wait until 1986 for me to enter, while marriage and the arrival of three daughters intervened. The sense of adventure had not left me, so the trek into the western sunset continued. The plan was to meet up again with a couple of my Torontonian friends in Gas Town, Vancouver, British Columbia. Instead we had staggered arrivals in Winnipeg, the "Gateway to the West." The train journey from Toronto, Ontario, to Winnipeg, Manitoba, as I was to discover, only takes a day and a half!

Mind you, while living in Toronto, but intending to move to Calgary, I had previously made a very brief sally farther west beyond Manitoba and Saskatchewan into the Province of Alberta. Calgary, Alberta, sits on the foothills of the Rockies. The Rocky Mountains were like nothing I had seen in Scotland. Viewed from Calgary, the repetitive snow peaks reminded me a little of the revolving passing background in a Yogi Bear cartoon! I returned "back east" to Toronto after only a week or so "out west."

I managed to hitch a lift back to Ontario with a young man and his girlfriend travelling back to Hamilton. He had come out west to Alberta in the same batch of travelers I came with. He was happy to have me share the driving. He had one of those three "cool" cars that all the kids in the '70s were into: Firebird, Trans Am, and Camaro. His was a Camaro, and I was to discover the hard way, that it wasn't designed for three people travelling a long journey with a pile of luggage in the back. I did manage to catch a little shuteye (though not while driving!) as we travelled through Montana, North Dakota, Minnesota, Wisconsin, across the long Mackinaw Bridge in Michigan, and back into Ontario.

The October scenery was glorious, and the people we met in "small-town USA" were the friendliest and most hospitable ever. The owner of a garage near Grayling, Michigan, put us up at his place for the night after we had pushed our broken-down car into his workshop. The job was too big, and needed to be started in the morning. The plan was that the garage owner would let the sojourners use his mechanic's equipment, free of charge!

I had the sleeping bag on the floor. I'll never forget the moment when his pet cat – who was missing a front paw – walked across my face in the middle of the night. Asleep and not knowing what was happening, I instinctively swatted it away, sending it several feet across the room. Well, the cat made a commotion that awakened the whole house! The owner accepted my humble apology for slapping his cat; he must have, for we dined on a hearty breakfast provided by his wife. I have never been very fond of cats, especially one who walks across your face in the middle of the night with a stumpy foot!

It took hours to repair the car. "This part" had to be taken off in order to gain access to "that part." A new word entered my vocabulary that day – a word I had not noticed in Scotland: *sprocket*. The Canadian I was with compared notes with the American garage owner regarding differences they perceived in their accents. I hadn't been in Canada long enough. To my untrained ear, they both sounded the same! At last, with sprocket repaired, we were on our way again. American hospitality is hard to beat anywhere!

Back in Toronto, a collapsed lung put me under the influence of an anaesthetic in the North York General as they operated on me during the Christmas and Hogmanay period of 1978–79. I remember the first words I spoke as the anaesthetic began to leave me: "I am *compos mentis!*" (mentally sound or sane). God then sent an "angel" to minister to me in the form of a Scottish nurse. She even made sure I received my "medicinal" dram daily! She was just about to return to Scotland for a well-earned holiday. So kind and thoughtful was this woman that, upon her arrival in Scotland, she phoned my mum to tell her that my recovery was going well.

After a month's stay in the hospital, it was full circle back to Scotland for me also – to convalesce in February and March of 1979. I returned again to Scotland in November of the same year for six months. Could this brief return to Scotland have been planned and directed by God? For it was in November 1979 that I met the woman who was to become my wife....

    1) God moves in a mysterious way,
          His wonders to perform;
          He plants His footsteps in the sea,
          And rides upon the storm.

    3) Ye fearful saints, fresh courage take;
          The clouds ye so much dread
          Are big with mercy, and shall break
          In blessings on your head.

6) Blind unbelief is sure to err,
And scan His work in vain;
God is His own interpreter,
And He will make it plain.

— William Cowper (1731–1800)
Hymn 31, RCH

Hudson's Bay Company

THE Red River flows north from Minnesota and North Dakota into Manitoba, where it bleeds into Lake Winnipeg. Manitoba's largest city, Winnipeg, has its fair share of Masonic lodges and Masonic historical connections. Owing to the vast flatness of the prairie, the City of Winnipeg is like a point within a circle encompassed by the horizon – there is not a hill in sight to speak of. In fact, the largest hills may well be the winter snow berms lining her streets and roads, many of which are named after Scottish Highlanders and French Voyageurs of bygone fur-trapping days.

Hudson's Bay Company was still a big concern when I arrived in Manitoba. The department store had a huge outlet on wide Portage Avenue. The history of Hudson's Bay Company reads like a Boy's Own Adventure novel! These were a mix of French Canadian voyageurs and Scottish Highlander fur-trappers who endured winter's grueling minus-forty-degrees temperatures, outsmarted or outran hostile natives, shot the rapids on rivers such as the Nelson, Columbia, McKenzie, and Fraser, and portaged between lakes through wolf and grizzly-bear habitat. Canoeing though grizzly-bear fishing spots would not be for the faint-hearted!

Speaking of a sense of adventure, Finan McDonald was, perhaps, one of the most colourful employees the Montreal-based North West Company ever had. Called Nor'Westers, these employees were in fierce competition with Hudson's Bay Company staff. The tension was eventually resolved by their amalgamation with Hudson's Bay Company in 1821. McDonald's family left Knoydart – which some call The Last Wilderness of Scotland – for North America in the late 1700s, when he was a slip of a lad. After his arrival, McDonald grew in stature and notoriety:

> His appearance was very striking.... In height he was six feet four inches, with broad shoulders, large bushy whiskers and red hair which, for some years, had not felt the scissors and which, sometimes falling over his face and shoulders, gave to his countenance a wild and uncouth appearance.
>
> Since one of his more talked-about feats turned on his having wrestled a buffalo bull which had tried to gore him, Finan's strength was clearly in proportion to his size. And his temper, it seems, was as fiery as his hair – there being more than one report of his having duelled with men who had allegedly insulted him. But for all that his fellow Nor'Westers were inclined to make mock of the "ludicrous melange of Gaelic, English, French and half-a-dozen Indian dialects" into which Finan tended to lapse when infuriated by some suspected slight, they were entirely appreciative of his undoubted ability – as signalled by his fluency in "Indian dialects" – to get along with the Columbia country's native peoples. And among these peoples, it appears, Finan's particular favourites were the Flathead, or Salish.... McDonald frequently, for the mere love of fighting, accompanied Flatheads in their war excursions against the Blackfeet. His eminent bravery endeared him to the whole tribe, and in all matters relating to warfare his word was law.
>
> (James Hunter, *Glencoe and the Indians*,
> Scotland: Mainstream Publishing, 1997, 92)

Two arteries in Winnipeg are MacGillivray Boulevard and Lagimodiere Highway, named after William MacGillivray (1764–1825) and Jean-Baptiste Lagimodière (1778–1855) both of whom worked for Hudson's Bay Company. Manitoba and Quebec are on opposite shores of the vast Hudson Bay, so it was only natural that Manitoba would have an influx of visitors from the more populous and settled Quebec. Lagimodière is the grandfather of the famous Métis leader Louis Riel (1844–1885) who helped stage the Red River Uprising. "The Métis Nation consists of descendants of marriages of Woodland Cree, Ojibway, Saulteaux, and Menominee aboriginals to French Canadian and/or Celtic settlers. Their history dates to the mid-seventeenth century."* The Festival du Voyageur is celebrated each February at St. Boniface, Winnipeg, to commemorate the Voyageur contribution.**

But there is also a Masonic connection to the North West Company and Hudson's Bay Company:

> Simon McGillivray, the second P[rovincial] G[rand] M[aster] of Upper Canada, was born in Scotland at Stratherrick, Inverness, in 1783, the youngest son of Donald McGillivray and Anne McTavish. His uncle, Simon McTavish (1750–1804), was the founder of the North West Company, the celebrated fur-trading rival of Hudson's Bay Company. Simon McGillivray and his older brother William (1764–1825) were both associated with the Company, and eventually became partners in it, though Simon was lame, and unable to take an active part in the actual fur-trade. It was William for whom Fort William [Thunder Bay, Ontario] was named....
>
> Simon McGillivray negotiated a merger between the North West Company and Hudson's Bay Company, which took place in 1821. In 1822, as we have seen, he was made P.G.M. [Provincial Grand Master] of Upper Canada. A year later, no doubt at his suggestion, his brother William – a much less-experienced Mason – was appointed P.G.M. for Montreal and William Henry. The two McGillivrays attended the Quarterly Communication of Grand Lodges on June 1843 in their capacities as Provincial Grand Masters.
>
> (*Whence Come We? Freemasonry in Ontario 1764–1980*, Wallace McLeod, Freemasons: Grand Lodge of Ontario, 49)

---

*(The Métis Nation, www.answers.com).

**Western Canada's largest winter festival, literally translated as Festival of the Traveller, is an annual event that takes place in Winnipeg, Manitoba, Canada, during February. "Voyageur" refers to those who worked for a fur trading company and usually travelled by canoe. The event celebrates Canada's fur-trading past and unique French heritage through entertainment, arts and crafts, music, exhibits, and displays. Source: Wikipedia

Canada's first Prime Minister was affectionately known as the "Old Chieftain." His name was John Alexander MacDonald. Born in Glasgow, Scotland, on January 11, 1815, he came to Ontario in 1820. I wonder if, like me, he felt something of the same awe and wonder when he first arrived in Canada from Scotland. Like me, he was a Mason, but unlike me who merely repaired railway engines and box-cars, he was the driving force in building a transcontinental railway line to join the East to the West. An optimist, he is reported to have said, "When fortune empties her chamberpot on your head, smile— and say 'We are going to have a summer shower.'" He died in 1891.

Entered Apprenticeships

*W*INNIPEG was a well and truly settled place when I arrived and, being Scottish, I naturally hung around with other Scots and people of Scottish extraction. Mind you, many a great weekend evening was had at the premises of the Winnipeg Irish Association on Princess Street. There, many a great "sing-song" was entered into with all the deep dedication of a collective homesick heart. The Irish Tavern Singers (affectionately known as The Irish *Tabernacle* Singers) kept our Irish eyes smiling and our Scottish feet tapping. The Northern Irish I came in contact with tended to be mostly of Scottish extraction, too. Many of the club's members, including myself, worked at the Canadian National Railway yards in town or at the nearby Transcona and/or Symington yards.

While living in Scotland in the 1970s, I had learned to weld and bend pipes as part of my Marine Plumber Apprenticeship Training begun in Yarrow's Shipyard in Scotstoun, Glasgow. I moved from the shipyards and subsequently finished my apprenticeship as a Domestic Plumber in Alexandria, Dunbartonshire, in 1976. I much preferred bashing sheets of lead around chimneys on the roofs of old castles and the likes than filling large-bore steel pipes with sand, heating them till they were cherry red, and bending them in the smoky shipyard. Then, in 1977, I worked as a plumber (among other things) in Toronto, Ontario, before moving to Winnipeg, Manitoba, in 1980. But on account of the severity of the Winnipeg winters, I heeded the wise counsel to go for a warmer, "indoors" job. I spent the whole decade of the '80s working for the Canadian National Railway.

The smoke of the Transcona Car Shop, with its doors closed against the long, minus-forty-degree winters, still makes me cough. My subsequent time in the Motive Power Department somewhat compensated for my five-year "imprisonment" in the sledgehammer pounding, "huck-gun," thunder cracking, burning-torch fuming, grinder-spark-spraying maelstrom presided over by a whip-cracking foreman. At last I was delivered from my five-year-long living nightmare in the Transcona Car Shop!

Call it escapism if you will, but I did manage to write some song lyrics while dreaming of better times lang syne in bonnie Scotland as my face was tanned by gas-welding steel pipes with my head wedged in some hard-to-reach spaces of dirty old coal and boxcars. Here's a sample:

Bonnie Scotland, Here To Stay

Hey, mister blacksmith,
    I'll make you a deal,
Forge me a sword from
    yon fine Scottish steel,

I promise I'll use it to fight
    for our cause,
Maintain our kingdom
    and all our Scottish laws.

I'll scour this land in search of truth
    and freedom just the same,
I'll chase all those who dare oppose
    our country's precious name:

From the tip of the windswept Shetlands,
   To the braes o' Galloway,
Coast to coast, and every island,
   O Bonnie Scotland, here to stay.

Highland folk being driven
   from their hills that run so steep,
O, tell me this, what's more important,
   a culture or some sheep?

Lallan folk exchanging ploughs
   for a London paved with gold,
Join with me, and let's not be
   a nation bought and sold:

From the tip of the windswept Shetlands,
   To the braes o' Galloway,
Coast to coast, and every island,
   O Bonnie Scotland, here to stay.

Ben Nevis rises majestically,
   a monument to all
Our men who fell on the battlefields
   when duty paid its call,

Climb atop that lofty cairn,
   my ashes in your hand,
Sprinkle me into the breeze
   to drift throughout the land:

From the tip of the windswept Shetlands,
   To the braes o' Galloway,
Coast to coast, and every island,
   O Bonnie Scotland, here to stay.

"Fangs" of Conscience

THERE were two hotels whose bars tempted the railroad workers to cross over to the "wrong side of the tracks" – especially on payday! Located opposite the main gate, each of the hotels "cashed in" on cashing our paycheques by charging a small fee. They were seedy joints – the type that had "dancing" girls. How was a young man without the moral wherewithal supposed to shun such fleshpots?

Elbows bent while eyes squinted. Beer, cheer, and leer were the order of the day – though not necessarily in that order! Women encouraged men to behave badly, and men encouraged women to behave badly. Just as a serpent injects its deadly venom into its victim through sharp fangs, so the medicinal and liberal use of alcohol helped to numb the sting of the semi- and sometimes fully cauterized consciences of the hotel patrons.

I avoided heeding the wise counsel offered in the Good Book where it is written, "How can a young man cleanse his way? By taking heed according to Your Word. With my whole heart I have sought You; Oh, let me not wander from your commandments! Your Word have I hid in my heart, that I might not sin against You" (Ps. 119:9–11).

Initially I had wanted to join Freemasonry mostly out of curiosity. Now I wanted to enter because I was seeking God in answer to pangs of conscience. God seemed to be obscured from my view. Was He watching me "through the lattice"? Could I catch glimpses of Him "through the lattice"? Was He a personal God, someone I could talk to, or was He just some hidden and invisible force in the universe, like wind or gravity? Perhaps He was standing behind the wall of the lodge....

Further Solomonic Insight

*I*T'S funny how we are able to hear the voices of people we associated with in our past simply by parading their faces one by one across the catwalk of our minds. The voices of schoolteachers, friends, acquaintances, and neighbours from misty years ago are heard again simply by recalling their faces. Each face a voice, each voice a face.

These faces don't exist in a vacuum, however. The faces and voices are attached to events or set periods in our history – some good, and some bad. In other words, context helps us to remember faces and voices. For example, in the Song of Solomon, as soon as the Shulamite woman says, "The voice of my beloved!" she starts thinking, "Behold, he comes leaping upon the mountains, skipping upon the hills. My beloved is like a gazelle or a young stag." She hears her beloved's voice, and immediately she pictures him as a deer sprightly springing on the hilltops. Conversely, one could expect that seeing a deer sprightly springing on the hilltops would cause her to think of her beloved Solomon.

In our minds, voices are associated with faces, and faces with voices. Both are associated with other objects and events. Like the words and music of some great song, voices and faces and faces and voices are mysteriously, but beautifully and harmoniously intertwined and interconnected.

Shalom means peace. The names of both Solomon and the Shulamite are derived from this Hebrew word. Both sound peaceful. On a deeper level, Solomon's face is reflected in that of the Shulamite. The mere thought of his name or sound of his voice delights her. She delights in him, and he in her. These two are at perfect peace with each other. They are one – a harmonious relationship. Speaking of the word "shalom," it is worth mentioning that I found Herman Dooyeweerd's "Shalom Hypothesis" (www.dooy.salford.ac.uk/shalom.html) to be interesting and very thought provoking.

The Bible says that God's voice is heard and His face is seen everywhere in creation (Ps. 19; Rom. 1:20), and that there is nowhere we can flee in order to escape His voice and face (Ps. 139:7–10). By "voice" and "face," I mean that the things that God has made "speak" of Him and reveal something of His character and attributes. Therefore, God is not far from each one of us (Acts 17:27). But the Bible also teaches us that though we ought to delight in hearing His voice everywhere and seeing His face everywhere – we don't!

It all began when Adam and Eve disobeyed God in the Garden of Eden by eating the forbidden fruit, i.e., the fruit of the tree of the knowledge of good and evil. Once sin entered in, they were ashamed and hid from God when they heard His voice calling out to them.

The following verses illustrate our behaviour towards God: "Then the LORD God called to Adam and said to him, 'Where are you?' So he said, 'I heard Your voice in the garden, and I was afraid because I was naked; and I hid myself.' And He said, 'Who told you that you were naked? Have you eaten from the tree of which I commanded you that you should not eat?' Then the man said, 'The woman whom You gave to be with me, she gave me of the tree and I ate'" (Gen. 3:9–12).

Before they disobeyed God, Adam and Eve loved each other like Solomon and the Shulamite. And they loved God in return. But now the mere sound of His voice has them scurrying off to hide in fear. The Bible teaches that ever since then we, too, attempt to suppress the truth of God in unrighteousness. And how this all works out in our lives today is that we consider it a bad experience to be reminded of God, even when we see something of Him revealed, e.g., in the grace of a gazelle or a young stag leaping on a hillside! Nor do we like it when we see His face looking back at us in a beautiful rose. Instead of delighting in Him, we hide from Him, delighting ourselves only in the things He has made.

There is a friction, a disharmony between us – individually and collectively – and God. It is of our own doing. This friction has the tendency to work against us in every sphere of life, making our lives harder to live. It causes sweat to form on our collective brow in everything we put our hand to. Even during the night, we are fitful and unrested. But the Bible teaches us that God hasn't deserted us.

His voice is still calling to us, and His face is still seen in everything He has made. And every sphere of life – such as art, music, architecture, linguistics, politics, religion, philosophy, and anything else you can think of – is governed by the laws the Creator God has put in every sphere.

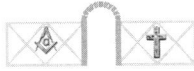

The Centre of the Universe

*I*T made very good sense to me (at the time!) that the place to find God would have to be the very centre of the universe. Find the centre of the universe and you will find God: Simple! But which universe? It seemed to me that there were all kinds of universes. Was God at the centre of the Philosophic universe? Or was He in the middle of the materialist universe? Perhaps He could be found at the centre of the scientific universe? Did Darwinist evolutionism have God at its centre? Surely for God to be God, He would need to be at the centre of every universe, including the physical one, because every "ism," it seemed to me, was based upon faith, i.e., faith in God and/or faith in some aspect of the God-ordered creation.

Where does the east end? Where does the west begin? How far is the east from the west? Does the sun really rise and set? The paradoxical thing about seeking God is that the seeker must start with himself. Yet, to seek God, the God-seeker must at the same time start with God. For who in their right mind would seek that which they believe does not exist? Even Darwin believed in the missing link he sought! And even though it may remain missing, today's Darwinist doesn't give up his faith in the theory of evolution – he just continually tweaks his theory!

When you think about it, to "seek" God, by definition, is to look for something which is lost to you. But the real paradox, as I was to discover, is seen with the realization that it is *we* who are lost, not God. I didn't know it at the time, but I was later to learn that the Bible teaches that the evidence for the existence of God is written on our hearts and consciences. Apparently, pangs of conscience are a sign of our "lost-ness." And, if you think about it, why would we set the bar so high that our consciences would accuse us for not measuring up to our own set of morals? Isn't our conscience a lot like a small policeman in our mind who blows a whistle to warn us when we are considering doing something wrong? Then he thumps on our door in the middle of the night to arrest us after we've broken the law. But whose law have we broken when we act against our conscience? Does each of us make up our own set of laws – the laws we continually break?

What I wanted to know was, who does the little policeman in our heads work for? And, anyway, who wants a policeman following them around all day and night? A boozy night of overindulgence only shuts him up till he slaps the morning "hangover handcuffs" on you. It would seem that to have your conscience work against you clearly illustrates that, one, you are not the author of the set of laws, and, two, you are not behaving in accordance with the Manufacturer's instructions. That was my own logical conclusion. But who was the Manufacturer? Was it Darwin's Time and Matter plus Chance? Or was there another? Was I, perhaps, catching glimpses of God showing Himself "through the lattice"?

As I strained and stretched my thinking, I noted that vice and virtue are not ideas that animals ponder. A lion doesn't wonder if it is morally right or wrong to eat a gazelle. He is driven to fill his belly to satisfy his pangs of hunger. A spider's conscience isn't keeping it awake at night with moral dilemma over catching flies. When a hamster devours its own young, it doesn't afterwards take to the bottle to dowse the flames of guilt! It has no conscience! Therefore, it suffers no guilty feelings. Why, then, are human beings stuck with an accusing conscience?

How do we know, inherently, that it is wrong to murder, lie, steal, and commit adultery? I concluded that it must be because each of us somehow must be the centre of the universe, which is to say that somehow God, or at least something of God, must be inherent in everyone. My big blunder in all of this reasoning was in my conclusion that if God is in each of us, then each of us must also be God! But then I began to wonder how this could be. For if collective humanity is God, then how can an individual human being be God? God would be incomplete without the collective whole and, thus, no longer God. And who made the universe in which all of us collectively and individually live?

> 1) All things bright and beautiful,
>   All creatures great and small,
>   All things wise and wonderful, –
>   The Lord God made them all.
>
> 6) He gave us eyes to see them,
>   and lips that we might tell
>   How great is God Almighty,
>   Who has made all things well.
>
> — Cecil Frances Alexander
> (1818–95)
> Hymn 18, RCH

The Braes o' My Childhood

*T*HE mountains of my childhood were woolly-white with the grazing sheep of summer and the sleeting snows of winter. Spring lambs grew quickly and before long looked like those that birthed them. Because of the way sheep use their teeth, the grassy spots on the hills were kept well mown. The sheep converted the grass into fertilizer with great efficiency. Sheep on a mountainside on a summer's day is a pretty picture – but seeing a stag glide across heather in any weather is something to behold!

I attended Levenvale Primary School with the local shepherd's sons. Come autumn, before the snow, it was time to get the sheep off the hills that overlooked Loch Lomond. Broad-shouldered Ben Lomond watched us from the other side of the loch. I would assist in the herding of the sheep, though the shepherd's two sheepdogs were far better at it than me! They were a joy to watch. The Border collie, Laddie, was the best, and made the other dog look stupid at times. A few whistles and, to us, incoherent calls from the shepherd would give Laddie the upper hand over the sheep. Mind you, I didn't appreciate the way Laddie would sneak up behind and bite my heels or backside! Ah, memories! I have fond memories of sheep and shepherds.

Solomon delighted in writing proverbs and songs speaking of trees, "from the cedar tree of Lebanon even to the hyssop that springs out of the wall," and he spoke also of animals, birds, "creeping things," and of fish. He would use the nature of things to illustrate deep spiritual truths. Jesus also used everyday objects and situations to teach spiritual truth. Jesus speaks of sheep and shepherds, likening His followers to sheep and Himself as a shepherd. He says:

> I am the good shepherd; and I know My sheep, and am known by My own.... And other sheep I have which are not of this fold; them also I must bring, and they will hear My voice; and there will be one flock and one shepherd. Therefore My Father loves Me, because I lay down My life that I may take

it again. No one takes it from Me, but I lay it down of Myself. I have the power to lay it down, and I have the power to take it again.... My sheep hear My voice, and I know them, and they follow Me. And I give them eternal life, and they shall never perish; neither shall anyone snatch them out of My hand. My Father, who has given them to Me, is greater than all; and no one is able to snatch them out of My Father's hand. I and My Father are one. (John 10:14–18; 27–30)

Thus, though I was deaf to it for some time, "The voice of my beloved," the Good Shepherd, by His Word and His Spirit, was calling even me! When God breathes out, the forest plays a wind-song on a thousand woodwinds, and so the Spirit soothes the heart of savage fallen man.

1) The Lord's my shepherd, I'll not want,
   He makes me down to lie
   In pastures green He leadeth me
   The quiet waters by.

2) My soul He doth restore again;
   And me to walk doth make
   Within the paths of righteousness,
   Ev'n for His own name's sake.

3) Yea, though I walk in death's dark vale,
   Yet will I fear none ill;
   For Thou art with me; and Thy rod
   And staff me comfort still.

   — Psalm 23, RCH

Colliding Universes

J CONSIDERED to be correct the view of Galileo and Copernicus that our sun is the centre of our solar system. But there are lots of suns (stars) in the night sky. So which of these stars is the centre of the material universe? This is where the Christian and Darwinist influences in my upbringing began to collide like anti-rhythmic clashing cymbals. My brain hemispheres began to take up the tension, just as east tugs west and the moon pulls on the tide.

I wrestled with these thoughts. Like the "Canada Arm" operating on the space shuttle in outer space, my mind began stretching out as I began groping for clues and answers. If Christian belief begins and ends with God, where does man fit in? And if Darwinian evolutionary belief begins and ends with man, where does God fit in? Did Jacob wrestle with God or a man?

In my head, the voice of Christianity put God at the centre of every sphere, while my inner evolutionary gruntings positioned me – or perhaps mankind – as the pinnacle of its universe. My "dead friend" who sits in the form of a book on a shelf among my other mostly "dead friends," says rather dogmatically: "Materialism and Darwinism are both historically and logically the result of philosophy, not of experimental science" (Herman Bavinck, *Reformed Dogmatics*, Vol. 2, Baker Academic, 518). After a great deal of thought – and whether I wished to admit it or not – to my mind, all belief systems (which includes scientific research) are based on faith. Thus, all systems of belief are founded on presuppositions. The theory of evolution cannot be proved empirically. It is simply a case of the "evidence" being made to conform to the prior assumption.

I loved science then and still do now. But science, true science, has not and cannot demonstrate to me that man created himself. Nor can it demonstrate to me how man or the material universe could evolve out of nothing. Nor can true science demonstrate to me how unthinking matter can become thinking matter. Where is the empirical evidence? Evolutionary belief is a philosophy. Therefore,

I had no problem with "science," per se, but with the atheistic scientific thinking that seeks to remove God from all its studies and conclusions.

I found that I didn't have enough faith to believe that *nothing* could become *something* without Almighty God. And, in the final analysis, I concluded that agnosticism is simply atheism for cowards! I wasn't brave enough to conclude that there is no God. Perhaps He's on the dark side of the moon. Perhaps He is at the bottom of the sea. Perhaps He is in the Masonic lodge!

The entire universe – every universe – needs to be explored before we can conclude there is no God. And what does the Bible mean where it states "But without faith it is impossible to please Him, for He who comes to God must believe that He is, and that He is a rewarder of those who diligently seek Him" (Heb. 11:6). It seems to me that the evolutionist is not seeking God in his sphere of activity. In fact, I get the distinct impression that evolutionary thought is a way of hiding from God! Therefore, the evolutionist must really be eating his bread in the sweat of his face!

For me, following the evolutionist view was like coming into the movie theatre in the middle of the movie. Because one wasn't there, one has to speculate what happened at the beginning by what one sees in the present. It helps a great deal if someone who was there at the beginning fills you in with some of the details. That way you are protected against drawing conclusions that might even be ridiculous.

I concluded that the atheist says there is no God because he already believes in his heart there is no God. Therefore, I concluded that I was not an atheist because I already believed that God is, even though I didn't personally know God at that time. But who and what is God, and where can God be found? One thing I did know was that He claimed to have been there in the beginning! "In the beginning God created the heaven and the earth. And the earth was without form, and void; and darkness was upon the face of the deep. And the Spirit of God moved upon the face of the waters. And God said, Let there be light: and there was light" (Gen. 1:1–3, KJV).

My conscience was telling me that God is. But in the words of

Agur, the son of Jakeh:

> Surely I am more stupid than any man, and do not have the
> understanding of a man. I neither learned wisdom nor have
> knowledge of the Holy One. Who has ascended into heaven,
> or descended? Who has gathered the wind in His fists? Who
> has bound the waters in a garment? Who has established all
> the ends of the earth? What is His name, and what is His
> Son's name, if you know? (Proverbs 30:2–4)

As a young man, though I had heard it often, I didn't "know"
God's name, nor did I know His Son's name. Christianity and evolutionism – I was tied to two powerful Clydesdale horses moving in
opposite directions. The education I received as a youth was pulling
me apart!

1) In the name of Jesus
   Every knee shall bow,
   Every tongue confess Him
   King of Glory now;
   'Tis the Father's pleasure
   we should call Him Lord,
   Who from the beginning
   was the mighty Word.

— Caroline Maria Noel
(1817–77)
Hymn 178, RCH

PART TWO

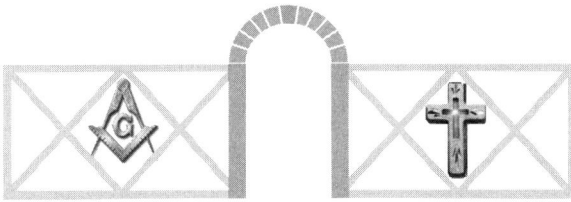

Masonry

Three Questions

I HAD known for some time that all Freemasons believe in a Supreme Being. For "Do you believe in the existence of a Supreme Being?" is the first of three questions asked of all petitioners seeking "Masonic light" ("light," in this case, means knowledge). The second and third are: "Do you believe that that Supreme Being will punish vice and reward virtue?" and, "Do you believe that that Supreme Being has revealed His will to man?" Each question must be answered satisfactorily in the affirmative or no entrance to the lodge at work can be gained.

It was upon anticipation of being asked if I believed in a Supreme Being that I personally began to deeply consider who and what God might be. What if I were asked to explain my understanding of God publicly to all the lodge members? Would I be able to articulate my belief?

As a candidate, I was later to discover, upon being asked these three questions, the Supreme Being of the Freemason is, (a) spoken of in the singular, (b) punishes vice and rewards virtue, and, (c) has revealed His will to man.

With these three questions answered in the affirmative at the door to the lodge, upon reflection, I had already discovered that the God of Freemasonry (and, therefore, the God I, too, believed in) could not be that distant "watchmaker" god of the deist, who supposedly created, and then – as with an old fob-watch – "wound up" the universe and left it running. I refused to be "fobbed off" with this view of God. The deist believes that his god only interacts (i.e., reacts) with creation (sometimes) when something goes wrong with it, but mostly stays very much hidden.

To me, deism separates man from God. Regarding deists, my dear "dead friend" says in one of his books: "A deist is a person who in his short life has not found the time to become an atheist" (Herman Bavinck quoting H. P. G. Quack, *Reformed Dogmatics*, Vol. 2, Baker Academic, 603).

I also could see that the God of Freemasonry, as well as not being the god of the deist, could not possibly be the pantheist god either. For the pantheist god is the god of the naturalist, i.e., the "all of nature is god" god, which god is simply the deist's god at a future stage of its "evolutionary" development!

Clearly then, the God of Freemasonry is not the god of the deist or the pantheist, for according to the questions posed at the door of the lodge – the God the Freemason believes in is (a) the Supreme Being, (b) called the personal "He" not the impersonal "it," and, (c) constantly interacting with His creation in that He punishes and rewards men according to their deeds, and, (d) He has already revealed His will to men.

It was my personal observation that in pantheism, God either is swallowed up by the world or the world is swallowed up by God. Either way, the serpent swallows its own tail, for God disappears in that God becomes nature and nature becomes God. Therefore, I concluded that the god of both pantheism and deism cannot be the God of Freemasonry because, according to its three questions, the God of Freemasonry is the Supreme Being who is a "He" and is therefore a Person, and He personally punishes vice and personally rewards virtue, and He has personally revealed His will to man. This God sounds very much like the living and true God who has revealed Himself in the sixty-six books of the Holy Bible!

I wish I had been asked these three questions about God sooner – even in my youth! That way I would have been compelled to think about the things of God sooner.

> In life's gay morn, when sprightly youth
>   with vital ardour glows,
> And shines in all the fairest charms
>   which beauty can disclose;
> Deep on thy soul, before its pow'rs
>   are yet by vice enslav'd,
> Be thy Creator's glorious name
>   and character engrav'd.
> For soon the shades of grief shall cloud
>   the sunshine of thy days;

And cares, and toils, in endless round,
  encompass all thy ways.
Soon shall thy heart the woes of age
  in mournful groans deplore,
And sadly muse on former joys,
  that now return no more.

— Ecclesiastes 12:1–4
Paraphrase 16, RCH

Punishing Vice and Rewarding Virtue

WHEN Masonry talks about taking a "good" man and making him "better," what is meant by the term a "good" man? I could see that the Apostle Paul in Romans 3 goes to great lengths to demonstrate that no one is "good" in the absolute sense of the word (see also Matt. 19:17). By this he means simply that all are fallen in Adam (Rom. 5:12). However, the Bible also speaks of certain men being "good" in the relative sense (e.g., Matt. 12:35).

Having understood the difference between absolute good and relative good, surely a "good" person may be one who believes in a Supreme Being who punishes vice and rewards virtue, in that He has already revealed His will to man. This, as it seems to me at least, is a good place to start, for it suggests that the person is not a law unto himself in that he, (a) believes that there is a higher law than his own judgment, (b) is able to discern something of a difference between evil and good, and, (c) holds that the evil he does will not go unpunished.

Upon reflection upon the three questions, one gets the impression that the lodge candidate is expected already to be, or at the very least, to have already understood the basic tenets of Biblical Christianity. For the "Supreme Being" referred to at the door of the lodge is monotheistic, for He alone is "Supreme." There cannot, as a matter of course, be two or more "Supreme" Beings. The plural of "omnipotent" is an oxymoron (unless, of course, speaking of each of the three Persons in the Trinity)! This, of course, means that the lodge-door remains firmly closed to all atheists, and technically, to all pantheists. The lodge-door then, is open only to monotheists, which includes Christians, Muslims, and Jews. (Hindus and others might succeed in entering only after a certain amount of "spin.")

Also, if the "Supreme Being" punishes vice and rewards virtue, that Supreme Being must be able to see not only the outward actions, but also the inward thoughts, of a man in order to hold that man responsible or accountable for his actions, for some men, it appears, are able to fake virtue on a human level.

And finally, by holding that the Supreme Being has revealed His will to man, Masonry is declaring that the Supreme Being has written His will internally on man's heart (presumably when He created us), or has written His will in a Book accessible to man, or both.

A small stumbling block I met with needs to be mentioned at this point. It was to do with what I later discovered about the Masonic teaching that the Supreme Being "rewards virtue." It became clear to me that the God who has revealed Himself in the sixty-six books of the Bible clearly teaches that He punishes vice. However, as complex as this was to me, God rewarding virtue was surely an even more complex matter!

I discovered that the Bible speaks of *temporal* punishments and rewards as well as *eternal* punishments and rewards, and that these two must never be confused. Even a cursory reading of the Book of Job, for example, will illustrate the fact that God does not always temporally reward virtue and punish vice, but sometimes allows the opposite, as Job painfully discovered!

I never really had the impression that Masonry taught a way of salvation. If Masonry had taught me a way of salvation, I would have followed it to the letter. But if that were the case, why was I seeking

God when (if Masonry actually teaches a works-righteousness) I should have been focusing on my own self-righteous good works?

I wasn't trying to climb the ladder degree by degree to God in Heaven (as some non-Masons suggest Masonry teaches). One Manitoba Mason said it well, "The focus of Masonry has to do with our relationships with our fellow creatures and with our determination to live moral or righteous lives, not because we are persuaded that this brings salvation, but because we know that it is approved by God. That is reason enough." ("A Short Allegory" by M. D. Jardine.)*

As I was later to discover in my own life, God has revealed in the Bible, from cover to cover, that no one is able to earn the eternal reward of everlasting life in Heaven for virtue – and no one can gain everlasting life apart from Jesus Christ.

> What can wash away my sin?
>   Nothing but the blood of Jesus.
> What can make me whole again?
>   Nothing but the blood of Jesus.
> Oh! Precious is the flow
>   that makes me white as snow;
> no other fount I know,
>   nothing but the blood of Jesus.
>   – Robert Lowry (1826–99)

The Water of Pappert Well

*I*N the late 1950s when we arrived back in the Vale of Leven, Scotland, from Ontario, Canada, we lived at the foot of the hills on the opposite side of the valley from Tullichewan. Our place was in Napierston Terrace, just where Jamestown blended into Bonhill

---

* www.grandlodge.mb.ca/mrc_docs/GodsExam.pdf

proper. Along the ridge of the hills was an old drover's "road" that not so long ago was used for taking cattle and sheep to the railway junction and markets at Stirling. The drover's road was more like a path of short grass (kept well manicured and manured by the ubiquitous black-faced sheep) winding its way through gorse, ferns, and the obligatory heather.

When we were young my dad would often take my older brothers and me for walks along that road, Mum being with us on occasion. My dad would invariably have us stop to take in the view of the valley below, and also to take in three deep breaths of fresh air. We were taught that fresh air is good for you. But we were taught that so also was fresh water. There was a well – a ring of bright water coming up from the ground – on the hill somewhere just off the drover's path. It was called Pappert Well. The spring had a big dipping-ladle fastened to a rock by a solid cast-iron chain.

My dad would "psych us up" as we approached the well with him. He kept saying that there was never water anywhere in the world that tasted better than the water of Pappert Well! My dad was fit to be tied when we had worked up a hill-walking thirst and got to the well only to discover that the ladle had gone missing! Not to be outdone I was going to scoop up some water from the well in my hands. "No son, you'll spoil the taste with sweaty hands. Put your face to the water and drink."

My dad was right. It was the best-tasting water ever! As it glided down my throat it seemed to permeate my whole being and bubbled up within me bringing refreshment to every nook and cranny. Like a rain-shower in the desert it caused the dry, parched wilderness of my stomach to bloom!

I Don My Apron

$\mathcal{I}$N 1986, after a matter of months, I had gone through the first three degrees of Blue Lodge Freemasonry. Each degree built upon the one before: first Entered Apprentice, then Fellow Craft, followed by Master Mason. I subsequently also joined the Royal Arch branch of Freemasonry (known as "Chapter"). Only a Third degree or Master Mason may apply to join Chapter.

A couple of key phrases helped me in my personal search for God in the midst of the rituals of each of the degrees of Freemasonry as I went through them: (a) Freemasonry is a beautiful system of morality, veiled in allegory and illustrated by symbols. And, (b) According to Masonry, *geometry* and *masonry* were originally synonymous terms. In other words, Masonry teaches morality, (i.e., a system of the principles of right and wrong conduct) by use of allegory, symbols, and geometry. Therefore, all the furniture in a Masonic lodge, and everything done in a Masonic lodge has a deeper philosophical (and perhaps, spiritual) meaning.

I intently listened to, and enjoyed, the lectures given in each degree. I paid very close attention to every action in each of the allegorical "plays" in which I was involved. Builder's tools and other objects symbolized virtues. We were taught that vices were to be avoided. The Masonic apron was a workman's apron – perhaps reminiscent of Adam clothing himself with an "apron" of fig leaves in the Garden of Eden, and of the Lord God clothing him with animal skin (see Gen. 3:7; 21, KJV). The armed-with-a-sword Inner Guard at the door into the lodge is perhaps reminiscent of the guard and the flaming sword that kept fallen man out of the garden: "So He drove out the man; and He placed cherubim at the east of the garden of Eden, and a flaming sword which turned every way, to guard the way to the tree of life" (Gen. 3:24).

I began to research, write, and present articles on Masonry and its workings to my fellow lodge members. My first article was titled: "I Don My Apron." My lodge subsequently awarded me a Bible for

that and some future writing efforts. I began diligently reading my
first Bible....

The Book!

AMONG the introductory pages of "the Book" I had been
presented by my lodge were the following words: "The
Holy Bible containing the Old and New Testaments translated out
of the original tongues, and with the former translations diligently
compared and revised. The text conformable to that of the edition
of 1611, commonly known as the Authorized King James Version."

There were other pages with illustrations of King Solomon's Temple
and comments, questions, and answers pertaining to Masonry, but
what I had in my hands was God's complete written Word, i.e., His
"revealed will" to fallen man. The following exhortation, which I took
to heart, was included in its introductory pages:

> Take this great and simple Book, white with age yet new with
> the dew of each new morning, tested by the sorrowful and
> victorious experience of the centuries, rich in memories and
> wet with the tears of multitudes who walked this way before
> us – lay it to heart, love it, read it, and learn what life is, what
> it means to be a man; aye, learn that God hath made us for
> Himself, and unquiet are our hearts till they rest in Him.
> Make it your friend and teacher and you will know what Sir
> Walter Scott meant when, as he lay dying, he asked Lockhart
> to read to him. "From what book?" asked Lockhart, and Scott
> replied, "There is but one Book!"
>
> (R. W. and Rev. Joseph Fort Newton)

The "One and Many" Problem

ASONS hold to the optimistic teaching of a someday world-wide brotherhood of man under the Fatherhood of God, resting on the three Masonic pillars of Brotherly-love, Relief, and Truth. This hope is expressed in the song "A Man's a Man for A' That" by the Scottish Mason and poet Robert Burns (1759–1796) where he writes:

> Then let us pray that come it may
> (as come it will for a' that)
> That Sense and Worth, o'er a' the earth
> Shall bear the gree an' a' that.
> For a' that an' a' that
> It's coming yet for a' that
> That man to man, the world o'er
> Shall brithers be for a' that.

I loved Masonry for this! For, as corny as the hackneyed term is, I believed that Freemasonry properly promoted – could bring about world peace! A Mason can travel to any part of the world and walk into a lodge and be welcomed as a brother. He can meet on the level with kings and princes, prime ministers and presidents, for all meet on the level under the letter G at the altar in the centre of the lodge, whether Christian, Jew, Muslim, or whatever – peace and harmony in the lodge. I thought that the whole world could become an extension of the lodge! I was so excited about the very idea that I began to promote Freemasonry wherever I went and obliquely encouraged not a few good men to seek membership.

For me at that time, Masonry was the answer to the age old "one and many" problem. This problem can be observed in every field. The Family is one yet many, the Church is one yet many, and the State is one yet many. Mankind is one but made up of many individuals. There is "unity and diversity." While I continued to, as it were, gaze at my Beloved "gazing through the lattice," I thought Masonry could build unity in the diversity of mankind, at least, or mainly, in the area of religion.

I began to see that creation and the various spheres in creation, such as family, church, and state, the arts and sciences, politics, education, etc., is simply the Creator "showing Himself through the lattice." For, as I was later to discover, God is the original "one and many." He is the original "unity in diversity," for He is three Persons yet one God.

Only in the Triune God does the problem of the one and the many, unity and diversity, the general and the particular, etc. have equal ultimacy (Cornelius Van Til). In the Godhead the one does not lord it over the many, nor do the many lord it over the one. Both the one and the many are equally ultimate and in perfect harmony in the Triune God. Thus all of creation in general reflects its Creator, as does man in particular.

Directly related to the one and many problem is the problem of "the general and the particular." Masonry works best when God is left in the sphere of the general, and spoken of in general terms. An imbalance and disharmony is introduced to Masonry when the particulars of God are considered. In other words, the harmony of the lodge at work would be disturbed if the "triune-ness" of God were brought to the fore and specifically addressed. For then those who deny the Trinitarian Father, Son, and Holy Ghost (such as today's Jews, the Muslims, and the Sikhs, etc.) would be ostracized. Like my evolution/Christianity dichotomy, this obvious Masonic imbalance of speaking of God only in general terms (without any particulars) was eventually to develop into a major stumbling block for me personally, (though the Masonic offspring, the Chapter of the Royal Arch, with its open reference to Jesus Christ and the Trinity helped hold me to Masonry a while longer).

If we were to view Freemasonry in terms of the problem of the general and the particular, we could say that the Blue Lodge (where the first three Craft degrees are conferred) deals with the general, and that the Red Lodge (which includes the Chapter or Royal Arch) deals with the particular. In other words, the Blue Lodge operates in the sphere of the one, and the Red Lodge in the sphere of the many. It might be said that Blue Lodge Masonry focuses on unity while Red Lodge Masonry focuses on diversity.

With Christianity in mind, one Masonic writer briefly alludes to Royal Arch Masonry (which includes Chapter) and Blue Lodge or Craft Masonry (which includes only the first three degrees):

> The Royal Arch, which was a separate degree, could have reference to Christian religion, but the first three degrees were to have no external references to Christianity, and the reference to the Volume of Sacred Law would be limited to the Old Testament. This issue of "de-Christianizing" Masonry has not gone away. It crops up from time to time in articles in the A[rs] Q[uatuor] C[oronatorum] and it is really not my business to go into the arguments, save and except to say that by talking about "de-Christianizing" the authors are mis-describing the issue.
>
> The issue is that what the Duke of Sussex did was quite extraordinary not just in terms of Masonic history but more importantly in terms of English history at that time. By insisting that Masonry be completely inclusive, he was out of step with the body politic in England.
>
> (Mark S. Dwor, *Some Thoughts on the History of the Tracing Boards*, Centennial-King George Lodge 171, British Columbia, Canada, 1999, Internet)

The title "Duke of Sussex" died with the death of Augustus Frederick (1773–1843). He was the sixth son of King George III. Frederick was Grand Master of the United Grand Lodge of England 1813–43.

When we consider our culture now, clearly contemporary so-called "multiculturalism" is a branch of the same bough of philosophy that undergirded the Duke of Sussex's thinking. It calls for replacing the particulars such as laws, principles, and tenets of the society with watered down generalities such as post-modernist political-correctness – just as the Duke of Sussex did to Blue Lodge Masonry regarding God. Is making any society "all-inclusive" not a sawing off of the very branch that Western society is sitting on? In other words, it seems to me, that a multicultural society will inevitably eventually collapse under its own weight! For given time, its "many" cultures will lack the coherence or the "oneness" that is needed to hold any society together. To put it yet another way, it seems to me that any society built on the foundation of contemporary secular-humanist multiculturalism will, in time, begin to discover its own ever-increasing lack of identity.

When I lived in Canada, the (tongue-in-cheek) catchphrase was "our identity as Canadians is that we have no identity!" Loss of identity is a form of amnesia. The Triune-God-denying Karl Marx wrote: "A people without a heritage are easily persuaded." For Canada, amnesia happened because its multicultural maple tree toppled and fell on the heads of her people. The collapse of multiculturalism is evident in the fact that now Christians in Canada are being ostracized, and banished to, as it were, the Red Lodge. And the VOSL (i.e., the Holy Bible) in Canada is close to being banned by being declared "hate literature" by the legislative powers. But I say to all true patriots who love Canada, "God keep our land glorious and free!"

It's not hard to see that contemporary Western multiculturalism is un-Christian. In some cases (such as present day Canada), multiculturalism clearly can be seen very much to be an anti-Christian attempt to deal with the one and many problem faced by societies, especially in those ethnically diverse and religiously pluralistic nations such as Canada has become. And, since by definition culture is the externalization of religion, it was really only a matter of time before Christians (in those nations that have adopted non-Christian multiculturalism) would be discriminated against.

It's my opinion that most of contemporary multiculturalism is a syncretistic system of religion. For, as demonstrated by its rejection of the "culture of Christianity," Canadian multiculturalism, in the final analysis, is now atheistic. Canadian society has blurred the lines of distinction between the one and the many, creating a serious imbalance whereby "oneness" has usurped the "many." In the name of endorsing many cultures, it has established one humanistic and anti-Christian multi-culture. The one now has ultimacy over the many; unity is now lording over diversity.

In this, Canada essentially has adopted Eastern ways, becoming pantheistic and even Buddhist (where all is one and one is all). By kicking against the goads that prod us and point us to the Trinitarian revelation, Canada, now, as it was for man immediately after the fall, eats its bread in the sweat of its face. For Canada, at present, is labouring hard for the sake of the many while neglecting the one. She is withering on the vine. In time, no doubt, the pendulum will swing in the opposite direction to the point that I will no longer be a Scots-Canadian but a Canadian-Scot (or, who knows, maybe just a non-hyphenated Canadian). But surely the harmony of a nation is attained, sustained, and maintained by keeping the plumb line perfectly perpendicular – as in Trinitarian equal ultimacy.

Multiculturalism fails when it denies the equal ultimacy of the one and many, and places the many above the one, or vice versa. Therefore, all multicultural societies that do not have the Triune God (and His Law summarised by the Ten Commandments – which Law also is revelation of Himself) as their basis, will, as history attests, fail and eventually disintegrate. Non-Trinity-honouring and Godless contemporary multiculturalism is a serpent destined to swallow its own tail and disappear!

Thus, by insisting that Masonry be completely inclusive back in the early 1800s, the Duke of Sussex was way ahead of his time. He was essentially wheeling the "Trojan Horse" of contemporary anti-Trinitarian multiculturalism into the Masonic lodge.

National Anthems

*W*ITH the Western nations' predilection for adopting the latest trend blown in by eastern winds comes what is called "religious pluralism." It's my humble opinion that religious pluralism is a philosophy concocted in the minds of people who think all religions are valid. Thus, paradoxically, Christianized nations have to be de-Christianized in order for this secular humanistic thought to be properly implemented.

The present movement of intolerance against Christianity is seen clearly in places like America where prayer has been removed from schools and the Ten Commandments from the walls of law courts, etc. This illustrates that, in the opinion of those who seek to de-Christianize America, that Christianity is not a valid religion, and that it is, therefore, not equal to other religions.

National anthems tend to include acknowledgement of the past, reference to the present, while embracing hope for the future. No doubt, the following fourth verse of the American national anthem, "The Star Spangled Banner," will have to undergo a fair bit of revision by the revisionists in order to remove reference to its Christian past, and make it fit their desired world without God:

> Oh! thus be it ever, when freemen shall stand
>> Between their loved homes and the war's desolation,
> Blest with vict'ry and peace, may the Heav'n-rescued land
>> Praise the Pow'r that hath made and preserved us a nation!
> Then conquer we must, when our cause it is just,
> And this be our motto – "In God is our trust."
>> And the star-spangled banner in triumph shall wave
>> O'er the land of the free and the home of the brave.
>> – Francis Scott Key (1779–1843)

National Anthems tend to bring a tear of emotion to the eye, especially when the eye belongs to one far from his home and native land! Like everything else in my life, the Canadian National Anthem took on a deeper meaning after I became a Christian. For the Christian, reference to God in a nation's national hymn is a Western wind bringing blessing, a Chinook melting Alberta snow!

> O Canada! Our home and native land!
> True patriot love in all thy sons command.
> With glowing hearts we see thee rise,
> The True North strong and free!
> From far and wide,
> O Canada, we stand on guard for thee.
> God keep our land glorious and free!
> O Canada, we stand on guard for thee.
> O Canada, we stand on guard for thee.
>
> — Robert Stanley Weir (1856–1926)
> Official Lyrics of
> *The Canadian National Anthem*

Originally *O Canada* was a patriotic poem by Sir Adolphe-Basile Routhier, a Quebec judge. Many English versions have appeared, but the one, which was widely accepted, was written in 1908 by Justice Robert Stanley Weir, in honour of the 300th anniversary of the founding of Quebec City. The following are a couple of heart-stirring verses of Weir's version:

> 2) O Canada! Where pines and maples grow.
> Great prairies spread and lordly rivers flow.
> How dear to us thy broad domain,
> From East to Western Sea,
> Thou land of hope for all who toil!
> Thou True North, strong and free!
> O Canada, we stand on guard for thee.
> O Canada, we stand on guard for thee.
>
> 4) Ruler supreme, who hearest humble prayer,
> Hold our dominion within thy loving care;
> Help us to find, O God, in thee
> A lasting, rich reward,
> As waiting for the Better Day,
> We ever stand on guard.
> O Canada, we stand on guard for thee.
> O Canada, we stand on guard for thee.

The following is an English translation of the French version of *O Canada*:

> O Canada! Land of our forefathers
> Thy brow is wreathed with a glorious garland of flowers.
> As is thy arm ready to wield the sword,
> So also is it ready to carry the cross.
> Thy history is an epic of the most brilliant exploits.
> Thy valour steeped in faith
> Will protect our homes and our rights
> Will protect our homes and our rights.

It's such a shame that Canada would deny her own heritage and even consider banning the Bible as hate literature. O Canada, who will protect our homes and our rights when the Book upon whose teachings our nation's foundations rest is burned?

Sing up, you true patriots! Sing up!

Old and New Testaments, Red and Blue Lodges

DOES the Blue Lodge/Red Lodge not reflect the Bible somewhat? For speaking of the Old and New Testaments, it has been said that what is in the Old *concealed* is in the New *revealed* – what is *latent* in the Old is *patent* in the New. Are the Blue Lodge degrees, like the Old Testament, full of "types"? And do the Red Lodge degrees contain the "anti-types" of the "types" contained in the Blue Lodge degrees? Those who have gone through Red Lodge, are they not able to shine the light of those degrees upon the Blue Lodge and see more and, therefore, get more out of the Blue Lodge degrees? The analogy is that the New Testament is a spotlight illuminating the shadowy figures in the Old Testament.

But the important point that should not be missed is that the Blue Lodge, like the Old Testament, is not devoid or empty of what is contained in far greater and clearer detail in the Red Lodge, like the New Testament. Another way to explain is that the "egg" of the Old Testament hatches and the New Testament emerges, the Old Testament foundational structure has the penthouse placed on top with all its lofty and heavenly views. Viewed from this elevation is, then, the Red Lodge (and the New Testament) not that dormer window that illuminates the Temple interior?

I entered Freemasonry as part of the quest in my search for God. Not being satisfied with God in general and wanting to know Him in particular, I was therefore "forced" to deal with the claims of Jesus Christ. He claims that the whole Bible, both Old and New Testaments, is about Him. For after His resurrection, He met two of His disciples who had thought that the crucifixion was the end of Jesus. "Then He said to them, 'O foolish ones, and slow of heart to believe in all that the prophets have spoken! Ought not the Christ to have suffered these things and to enter into His glory?' And beginning at Moses and all the Prophets, He expounded to them in all the Scriptures the things concerning Himself" (Luke 24:25–27).

The Old Testament's sacrificial system was typical of Jesus. The Old Testament prophets, priests, and kings typified Jesus. The tree of life, and Noah's ark are pictures of Him. Old Testament Circumcision and Passover pointed to Him – i.e., "the Lamb of God who takes away the sin of the world!" (John 1:29). The Temple and all its furniture are typological of Jesus Christ. Through all these real and historical events, am I able to see Jesus Christ? In looking through the lattice, I could see Him in the shadows of the Blue Lodge, but I saw Him more clearly in the Red Lodge.

The Masonic Temple

*A*s one might expect when looking at Masonry – which has to do with "building" – geometrically, the Masonic Temple is the shape of a brick (i.e., a right-angle parallelepipedon, which is a 6-faced polyhedron all of whose faces are parallelograms lying in pairs of parallel planes). However, the lodge's starry ceiling symbolizes that it extends from earth to Heaven, the dwelling place of God. God is referred to in Blue Lodge Masonry as the Grand Geometrician of the Universe, among other "general" titles. The all-seeing eye of God-above watches man-below in all his undertakings.

The lodge represents Solomon's Temple in the process of being built, which in turn reflects the heart of the "good" man being made better by Masonic teaching. The Volume of the Sacred Law, i.e., God's "revealed will," sits open on an altar in the middle of the lodge when the lodge is "at work." As God's revealed will rests in the centre of the lodge, so it is to also "lodge" in the Mason's heart.

The Psalmist, under inspiration of the Holy Ghost, says: "Your word I have hidden in my heart, that I might not sin against You" (Ps. 119:11). The Holy Ghost moved the Apostle Paul to say to Christians, "Do you not know that you are the temple of God and that the Spirit of God dwells in you? If anyone defiles the temple of God, God will destroy him. For the temple of God is holy, which temple you are" (1 Cor. 3:16–17). As well as being likened to the temple of God, the Mason is also likened to a brick or stone in the Temple, a rough ashlar – i.e., a roughly hewn stone in need of dressing, as in "you also, as living stones, are being built up a spiritual house, a holy priesthood, to offer up spiritual sacrifices acceptable to God through Jesus Christ" (1 Pet. 2:5).

Hiram, the widow's son, who was "filled with wisdom and understanding and skill in working with all kinds of bronze work" (1 Kings 7:14) made the two bronze pillars that stood at the entrance of Solomon's Temple. This Hiram figures prominently in the Blue Lodge's Third degree. He has the title of Hiram Abif. The "Abif" appellation is no doubt taken from 2 Chronicles 2:13 where Hiram, king of Tyre, refers to Hiram the craftsman, in the original Hebrew as Huram Abi (literally "Hiram, my father"). The term "my father" is a title of honour Hiram the king bestowed upon Hiram the craftsman.

The Puritan Thomas Manton, who was asked to write a commendatory preface to the famous 1647 Westminster Catechism used by Presbyterians the world over, said:

> It is a great relief to faith to consider that God is able to keep us. Accordingly, you find it urged in Scripture (see John 10:28–29; 1 Pet. 1:5; Rom. 14:4), "He shall be holden up, for God is able to make him stand." The two pillars of the temple were Boaz and Jachin, Strength, and He will establish; the power of God and the mercy of God are the two pillars upon which our confidence standeth.

As a new Mason, I knew something of the "power of God" by contemplating the stars in their courses. But what was the "mercy of God"? Where should I look to see that? Knowledge of the mercy of God would have to wait! As I looked at the entrance into Solomon's Temple – and as I peered into my own heart – I penned the following (and, if you look closely, you should be able to make out the names of the two pillars):

In Strength

Be humble and meek,
    as a mouse, rustle among the Leaves.
Open your heart,
    as a man that ever believes.
And pray that the Word,
    on your heart is embossed.
Zealously seek, for that which was lost.

He Will Establish

Justice prevails when all else fails,
    for God's will will always be done;
A mighty Flood, a splash of Blood,
    or the total eclipse of the sun.
Chance plays little part
    when you know in your heart

a catastrophe would have been prevented,
Had faith been applied
    instead of denied
    and wickedness never invented.
In Strength shall we find the Established Design
    with Stability once more elected.
Never again will the folly of men
    tear down what God has erected.

Post Tenebras Lux
(After Darkness, Light)

*T*HE Reformation began with Martin Luther (1483–1546) nailing The Ninety-Five Theses to the door of All Saints' Church in Wittenberg on October 31, 1517. He wanted the Church, which had become terribly corrupt, to reform her ways. He was no mean theologian, but if Martin Luther was the "brawn" of the Reformation, then John Calvin (1509–1564) was the "brain."

John Calvin was a second-generation Reformer. He carefully and consciously built upon the solid foundations laid by Martin Luther and Ulrich Zwingli. Calvin looked with great respect to Luther as his father in the Faith. Luther was very aware of the up-and-coming distinguished scholar and author, John Calvin, and praised his *Institutes*. However, while their foundations were the same, Luther's central focus was justification by faith, whereas Calvin's focus was primarily the sovereignty of God. These Reformers shared an overwhelming sense of the majesty of God. Luther focused on the miracle of forgiveness, while Calvin went on to give the assurance of the impregnability of God's purpose. If Luther's central Biblical text was "The just shall live by faith," Calvin's was "Thy will be done on earth

PART TWO — *Masonry*

as it is in Heaven." (www.reformationsa.org/celebrate_refor
mation_calvin.htm).

Whereas Luther cranked the handle that brought the Reformation
to life, Calvin got up a head of steam and started the slow-moving
and somewhat cumbersome railway engine of Calvinism. The fire lit
at the time of the Reformation is that which burns under Calvinism's
huge boiler. Calvinism has rolled unstoppably on track through the
centuries.

Luther pointed to the corruption that had crept into the Lord's
Church and he wanted it stopped. Calvin subsequently brought an
ordered understanding to how God's Word applies to every area of
human life, including family, church, state, and every related sphere.
Thus the Dark Ages ended with the light that dawned and rose with
the Reformation. The Reformation took firm hold when the people
of Europe finally held the Word of God in their own hands and
in their own language. Thus, Christ and His Gospel set alight the
whole of Europe!

During the Dark Ages, the corrupted Romanized church had obscured God from the sight of the people by imposing itself, like the
thick veil in the Temple, between men and God. This led to all manner
of corruption as evil priests and others took advantage of the widely
held belief of the people that their souls were in the hands of – and
therefore at the mercy of – the church. Luther and Calvin could see
that it wasn't the church, but rather Jesus Christ who was the Saviour
of men. They saw clearly that the church was merely the instrument
for the proclamation and affirmation of this truth to all believers.

I have since learned what the Reformers learned at the time of
the Reformation, namely, that Christ is the Light of the World, and
that His Word, the Bible, is the revelation that salvation is by grace
alone, through faith alone, in Christ alone, according to the Word
alone, to the glory of God alone.

> 1) A safe stronghold our God is still,
>   A trusty shield and weapon;
>   He'll help us clear from all the ill
>   That hath us now o'ertaken.

The ancient prince of hell
Hath risen with purpose fell;
Strong mail of craft and power
He weareth in this hour;
On earth is not his fellow.

2) With force of arms we nothing can,
Full soon were we down-ridden;
But for us fights the proper Man,
Whom God Himself hath bidden.
Ask ye who is this same?
Christ Jesus is His Name,
The Lord Sabaoth's Son;
He, and no other one,
Shall conquer in the battle.

— Martin Luther (1483–1546)
Translated from the original German
by Thomas Carlyle (1795–1881)
Hymn 526, RCH

The Letter G

MY own personal "reformation" began as I studied the Bible I had been given by my lodge. However, I found the archaic English of the King James Version a hindrance; it was very difficult to read. But with Bible in one hand and dictionary in the other, I persevered! And just as everything in the lodge revolved around the letter G that hangs from the ceiling above the open Bible on the altar, so my whole life began to revolve around God and His Word. And like the circumambulations in the lodge, I was to wander in circles before I was to kneel before the Almighty and cry out to Him for light and life.

What does the hanging letter G represent?

There are two distinct meaning[s] given for the letter G: the first is for Geometry, and the second is for God. This is very clear in the two different versions given for it, as outlined in the Second Degree work. At the end of the Tracing Board lecture in the Second Degree, the following statement occurs, in reference to the seven who make the Lodge perfect: They have likewise an allusion to the seven liberal arts and sciences, namely grammar, rhetoric, logic, arithmetic, geometry, music, and astronomy. The Tracing Board lecture then concludes with the following: After our ancient brethren had gained the summit of the winding staircase, they passed into the middle chamber of the temple where their attention was directed to certain Hebrew characters which are depicted in a Fellow Craft Lodge by the letter G, denoting God, the Grand Geometrician of the Universe to whom we must all submit and whom we ought to humbly adore. (Mark Dwor, *The Letter* G, Centennial King George Lodge 171, British Columbia, Canada, 1998; www.freemasonry.bcy.ca/texts/address.html)

Circling God

At the time I began contemplating the teachings of Masonry during the late 1980s, I was employed by the Canadian National Railway. I owned the house in which I lived with my wife and three daughters, and I had a decent car in the driveway. But I began to wonder if that was all there was. Live, then die? What was life really all about? – the propagation of the species? I began to think about life, death, and God more deeply. Was I looking at God looking at me through the lattice? Would God come out from behind the lattice to a place where I could clearly see Him? The more I realized how lost I was, the more I cried out to the Almighty. But, for now, I would have to content myself with just a "general" knowledge of God. The "particular" would come later. I wrote,

He comes to me
    When I hear the church-bell ringing
    When the blackbird keeps on singing
    As I face eternity.
I see His hand
    In a feather from a seagull
    On the wingtip of an eagle
    As it soars across the land.
He comes to me
    When I hear the children playing
    And on my knees when I am praying
    When His Word speaks to me.
O praise His name
    For the gift of my salvation
    Every creature in creation
    On bended knee.
O praise His name
    To the Father be all glory
    He's the author of His story
    He's the One who set me free!

Solomonic Insight

IN Song of Solomon, the beautiful Shulamite says, "The voice of my beloved! Behold, he comes leaping upon the mountains, Skipping upon the hills. My beloved is like a gazelle or a young stag." Lovely picture painted by words! But what are words? Aren't words symbols, a series of noises we make in order to communicate to others some image we hold in our mind?

Even the written word is a series of symbols designed to convey thought. Of course the person receiving the information needs to have a treasury of memories (i.e., a previous knowledge, whether experienced personally or attained by other means) with which to access in order to relate to what is being communicated. It's a bit like needing the apparatus to play a DVD. If you don't have the wherewithal it's very difficult to understand what is being communicated. That's why it's hard to communicate abstract thought to little children. The Shulamite hears the voice of her beloved and the sound of his voice causes her to picture him as a young stag gracefully bounding over hills. His voice triggers a memory of the way she perceives her beloved.

It has been my observation that other things as well as words spoken or written can communicate information. For instance, smells can trigger thoughts where we recall faces and voices and even replay events from the past. Sometimes that which triggers the memory is subliminal. One time Dorothy and I were at a social evening in the Irish Club in Winnipeg, and were sitting next to a married couple. The husband was a Scot and his wife was Canadian. As we talked with them, my mind began to drift to events from my childhood.

There I was, a young lad growing up in Scotland. During the school summer holidays I would spend many hours alone, wandering the hills above Loch Lomond. The thick woodland with its damp earthy smells gave way to the fresh air of heather-clad hills. The trees were assorted, with pine, hazel, sycamore, oak, and the silver bark of birch standing out like markers along the way. Flowering rhododendrons set the mood. Brambles and sometimes raspberries assuaged any slight hunger pangs I might have had along the way.

The cooing of the big woodpigeons would bring me soothing comfort in the woods, even though their sweet voices would invariably end abruptly as if someone had interrupted them. The calls of the grouse to one another on the higher moor were teasing, as they stayed hidden from sight. When disturbed, the very heather itself became like an electrically charged thundercloud as a covey of grouse scrambled to become airborne like WWII Spitfires. Capercailzies, larger cousins of the grouse, preferred to patrol the cool woods. One time I stumbled on a capercailzie and trembled as he, like an Indian chief on the warpath, ruffled feathers and all, screeched his battle cry at me!

Another time I was walking along a country lane when I heard a weird kind of barking noise. Then crashing out of the bushes came this huge red deer stag tossing his great rack of antlers into the fear-filled air. I don't know which of us was the more surprised to see the other, him or me! I thought I was in for it as he barked disdain in my direction! But off he went bounding up the hill like the deer he was.

Mostly red deer and the smaller roe crossed my path in my youth. It was sheer delight to watch them gracefully bounding across a farmer's field and leap the fence at the edge of it as if on legs of steel springs. Once when I was near the Vale of Leven hospital I saw an albino stag with silent speed gliding eerily across a field at dusk. The fence it was approaching was very high, but it cleared it effortlessly and my mouth fell open in awe.

I was probably about 10 or 11 years old when I started singing the following while walking the woods and hills of home, often kilt-clad:

> Run like a deer, run like a deer,
> Over the hills, over the hills.
> If only I could run like a deer.

Meanwhile, returning to the present at the Irish Club, I began to notice that the Canadian woman at our table was wearing a lovely-smelling perfume. I complimented her on it and asked what it was called. She replied, "A Walk in the Woods."

Who Is the Supreme Being?

ANTICIPATING being asked if I believed in a Supreme Being, I had been asking myself who or what was the Supreme Being I purported to believe in. God could not possibly be the old man with the long white beard sitting on a cloud that had popped into my mind when I first began to contemplate this. I discovered that though I believed in God, I didn't really "know" God. The Bible says, "You believe that there is one God. You do well. Even the demons believe – and tremble!" (James 2:19). Obviously, there must be more to believing in God than just acknowledging His existence! Else why do the demons tremble? And why are they not permitted to enter into Heaven, if "believing in God" is enough?

I worked beside some men in the railway who called themselves Jehovah's Witnesses. We used to have some great theological conversations as we took apart and rebuilt diesel train engines. As I read my Bible, I began asking them to explain things for me. The main thing I wanted to know was if Jesus was Jehovah. They were very insistent that He was not. My response was, then why would Jesus say He was? "I give them eternal life...I and the Father are one" (John 10:28a, 30). We need only to look at the Jews' reaction to His claim: They moved to stone him in accordance with Mosaic Law (Lev. 24:15) saying, "We [stone you]...for blasphemy, because You, being a man, make Yourself God" (John 10:33). In another example, Jesus said, "Most assuredly, I say to you, before Abraham was, I AM!" (John 8:58). Jesus used the very name that the Holy LORD revealed to Moses at the burning bush. "God said to Moses, 'I AM WHO I AM. Tell them I AM has sent me to you.'" (Ex. 3:14). The immediate reaction of the Jews was, once again, to stone Him for blasphemy (John 8:59). It is clear that Jesus, speaking plainly, claims to be God.

The Jehovah's Witnesses gave me their own New World Translation of the Holy Scriptures (NWT, Revised 1984). I took it home and studied it, finding the New World Translation language far easier reading than the word sequences and archaisms of King James English in the Bible the lodge had presented me!

Using the New World Translation, we considered the following words – of interest to every Mason – found in Isaiah 8:13-15: "Jehovah of armies – he is the One whom you should treat as holy, and he should be the object of YOUR fear, and he should be the One causing you to tremble. And he must become as a sacred place; but as a stone to strike against and as a rock over which to stumble to both the houses of Israel, as a trap and as a snare to the inhabitants of Jerusalem. And many among them will be certain to stumble and to fall and be broken, and to be snared and caught."

I noticed in these verses that Jehovah Himself was to become the "stone." If Jehovah is not the same Person as Jesus Christ then I wondered why His Apostle Peter wrote the following:

> Coming to him [the Lord Jesus] as to a living stone, rejected, it is true, by men, but chosen, precious, with God, you yourselves also as living stones are being built up a spiritual house for the purpose of a holy priesthood, to offer up spiritual sacrifices acceptable to God through Jesus Christ. For it is contained in Scripture: "Look! I am laying in Zion a stone, chosen, a foundation cornerstone, precious; and no one exercising faith in it will by any means come to disappointment."
>
> It is to you, therefore, that he is precious, because you are believers; but to those not believing, "the identical stone the builders rejected has become [the] head of [the] corner," and "a stone of stumbling and a rock-mass of offense." These are stumbling because they are disobedient to the word. To this very end they were also appointed. (1 Pet. 2:4–8, NWT)

I could see that in Jesus Christ's day, Jehovah had become to unbelieving Jews what He through His Prophet Isaiah said He would become: a stone of stumbling and a rock of offence. Indeed, even so-called Jehovah's Witnesses would agree that Isaiah is speaking of Jesus in the following well-known passage, "He is despised and rejected of men; a man of sorrows, and acquainted with grief: and we hid as it were our faces from Him; He was despised, and we esteemed Him not" (Isa. 53:3, KJV). Therefore, Jehovah Himself is Jesus! And the Lord Jesus through His Apostle Peter is urging believers to put their faith in Him, i.e., "The stone that the builders rejected has become the head of the corner. This has come to be from Jehovah himself; It is wonderful in our eyes" (Ps. 118:22–23, NWT).

Jesus is "the stone" that the builders rejected, He is the rock of offence, for He says to the scribes and Pharisees who were trying to kill Him,

Did you ever read in the Scriptures, "The stone that the builders rejected is the one that has become the chief cornerstone.
From Jehovah this has come to be, and it is marvellous in
our eyes"? This is why I say to YOU, The kingdom of God will
be taken from YOU and given to a nation producing its fruits.
Also, the person falling upon this stone will be shattered. As
for anyone upon whom it falls, it will pulverize him. (Matt.
21:42–44, NWT)

That Jesus is Jehovah was even more confirmed to me when I
learned that the Apostle Paul says that "the rock" that was with
Old Testament Israel in the wilderness was Christ, i.e., the rock that
Moses struck and from which water flowed, symbolizing Christ's real
presence with them (Ex. 17:6; Num. 20:11).

The New World Translation of the Holy Scriptures records Jehovah
saying these words: "Does there exist a God besides me? No, there
is no Rock. I have recognized none" (Isa. 44:8b, NWT). The New King
James Version accurately renders the same, "Is there a God besides
Me? Indeed there is no other Rock; I know not one." And, in her
prayer, Hannah echoes the same, in the First Book of Samuel, "No
one is like the LORD, for there is none besides You, nor is there any
rock like our God" (1 Sam. 2:2). The Jehovah's Witnesses version of
the Bible proclaims the same, "There is no one holy like Jehovah, for
there is no one but you; And there is no rock like our God" (1 Sam.
2:2, NWT). The New World Translation of Psalm 18:31 clinches it for
me: "For who is a God besides Jehovah? And who is a rock except
our God?" (Ps. 18:31, NWT). Indeed! And when it is all put together, in
the words the Apostle Thomas exclaimed to and of the resurrected
Jesus Christ, "My Lord and my God!" (John 20:28).

My Jehovah's Witnesses workmates said they would have to check
with their church elders and report back to me on the meaning
of the Isaiah 8:13–15 passage. Subsequently, they told me that this
passage did not refer to Christ, but was fulfilled before the time of
Christ in some other way. Very much dissatisfied with their answer
from the plain and clear reading of the Bible, I became convinced
intellectually that Jesus Christ is the manifestation in the flesh of the

LORD God or Jehovah Elohim, the Supreme Being who alone is the stone that the builders rejected, the Rock. However, I also needed to become convinced of this in my heart, i.e., spiritually.

The Trinity

I COULD see clearly that Jesus Christ was a stumbling block for my Jehovah's Witnesses workmates. They were happy to concede that Jesus was "a god" even "Mighty God" but not "Almighty God"! Indeed, it became clear to me that the so-called Jehovah's Witnesses have two gods: a "big god" they call "Jehovah" and a "little god" they call "Jesus" – neither of which, as I saw it, were the Jehovah and Jesus revealed in Scripture! An old "penny-farthing" bicycle springs to mind – a big wheel and a little wheel, a big god and a little god.

Apart from maybe omitting a comma, their New World Translation does well enough translating the Hebrew of Isaiah 9:6, which speaks of Jesus thus: "For there has been a child born to us;...and the princely rule will come to be upon his shoulder. And his name will be called Wonderful Counsellor, Mighty God, Eternal Father, Prince of Peace." However, it doesn't do so well translating the Greek of John 1:1-2, which also speaks of Jesus: "In [the] beginning the Word was, and the Word was with God, and the Word was *a* god." By insisting on using the words "a god" here, Jehovah's Witnesses are revisiting the ancient heresy of Arianism (a heresy that arose in the fourth century, which denied the Divinity of Jesus, named after Arius A.D. 250-336). The Nicene Creed 2.2* of A.D. 325, and slightly enlarged in 381, was written to refute Arius's claim that "the Son was the highest creation of God and thus essentially different from the Father" (*New Dictionary of Theology*, Edited by Sinclair B. Ferguson and David F. Wright. Downers Grove, IL: Inter-Varsity Press, 1988).

---

* See the Nicene Creed in Glossary, pp. 185–86.

It is very strange that my Jehovah's Witnesses workmates would believe that the Son of God, i.e., the Word, is a created being. For immediately following the very verses they were using to try to refute the Divinity of the Second Person in the Trinity, there is the following reference to the Word who became also flesh: "All things came into existence through him, and apart from him not even one thing came into existence" (John 1:3, NWT). Indeed! Yet, contrary to this verse of Scripture, the Jehovah's Witnesses insist that there was one thing that came into existence apart from the Word, i.e., the Word Himself!

I could see that something other than the plain reading of Scripture was driving my Jehovah Witnesses workmates to deny that God was Father, Son, and Holy Spirit – three equal but distinct Persons, yet one God. For didn't Jesus command His Church on earth to baptize the nations "in the name [singular] of the Father and of the Son and of the holy spirit"? (Matt. 28:19, NWT). Even the Jehovah's Witnesses' own version of the Bible, the New World Translation (NWT), testifies that the name (singular) of God is "Father, Son, and Holy Spirit." (See also Matt. 28:19.)

All names in the Bible given to God are a revelation of who God is. In Hebrew, generally speaking, "El" means "God"; "El Elyon" means "the Most High God"; "Elohim" means "the Triune God" (i.e., God in the plurality of at least three Persons); "Eloah" means "God" (in the singular); "Jehovah," usually rendered LORD, means "the personal name" of the Eternal God, the I AM; and "Jehovah Elohim," usually rendered LORD God, means "I AM the Triune God." These names have been designed by God to reveal to us something of who He is. Therefore, God's name "Father and Son and Holy Spirit" reveals the three Persons in the Godhead.

> 6) I bind unto myself the Name,
> The strong Name of the Trinity,
> By invocation of the same,
> The three in One, and One in Three,
> Of whom all nature hath creation,
> Eternal Father, Spirit, Word.

Praise to the Lord of my salvation:
Salvation is of Christ the Lord.

— St. Patrick (372–466)
Version by Cecil Frances
Alexander (1818–1895)
Hymn 506, RCH

A New Chapter

AFTER completing the three degrees of the Blue Lodge, I came to a fork in the road. Should I now seek admission into Scottish Rite or York Rite Freemasonry? I had read enough of the book, *The Morals and Dogma of the Ancient and Accepted Scottish Rite of Freemasonry* (1871), by the American, Albert Pike (1809–1892), to put me off taking the Scottish Rite route! Albert Pike is very much maligned by – and apparently very much misunderstood by – anti-Masons. I personally found the contents and language of his *Morals and Dogma* book to be very esoteric. I believe this in itself is an unchristian approach to writing, for Christianity is all about truth done in the light – nothing is purposely hidden. Thus the word "occultish" sums up Pike's book for me.

It was through reading *Morals and Dogma* that I was led to believe that there had to be an elite and occultist group – a wheel within the wheels of Masonry if you will – in which and among which the hidden secrets of God and His universe resided. For Pike unabashedly alleges that the Master Mason, after having gone through the first three degrees, has been duped. Wrote Pike:

> The Blue Degrees are but the outer court or portico of the Temple. Part of the symbols are displayed there to the Initiate, but he is intentionally misled by false interpretations. It is not intended that he shall understand them, but it is intended

that he shall imagine he understands them.

(Albert Pike, *Morals and Dogma of the Ancient and Accepted Scottish Rite of Freemasonry*, prepared for the Supreme Council of the Thirty-Third Degree for the Southern Jurisdiction of the U.S., Charleston, 1871, 819)

In other words, Pike was urging the Master Mason to proceed through the Scottish Rite degrees in order to learn and discern the true nature of Masonry.

At the time, what Pike had written seemed very ominous to me, especially in light of what Scripture has to say about occult practices! Indeed on Pike's instigation I started reading writings on the Jewish cabala. Thankfully, however, instead of going through the Scottish Rite, I sought and gained entrance into the "more Christian," as I was told, York Rite.

This being said about Albert Pike and his *Morals and Dogma*, and whatever terrible things his enemies may have said about him, Pike is reported to have been a staunch Trinitarian Christian till his dying day. I'll let the reader make up his or her own mind on this! There is much information about him to be found on the Internet that has been written by Freemasons themselves. The Scottish Rite, from what I could see, had very little if anything to do with Scotland — hence, for me, the obvious "Scottish" attraction was assuaged.

The Holy Royal Arch, or York Rite Freemasonry, is a branch of what is sometimes referred to as Red Lodge. The Holy Royal Arch is more commonly known as "Chapter." Royal Arch, or Chapter, is a continuation (even the completion) of the three Blue Lodge degrees, as has been well said: "Pure Ancient Freemasonry consists of but three degrees, that of Entered Apprentice, Fellowcraft, and Master Mason, including the Supreme Order of the Holy Royal Arch."*

A cursory search of the Internet revealed the following handy, concise, and verifiable information regarding Chapter:

> The Chapter of Royal Arch Masonry itself consists of four degrees: Mark Master; Past Master; Most Excellent Master, and Royal Arch Mason. The Royal Arch Degree being said to

---

* *Articles of Union*, Mother Grand Lodge (England), 1831.

be the climax of Ancient Craft Masonry and Masonic Symbolism. It is described as "the root and marrow of Freemasonry." It is the complete story of Jewish History during some of its darkest hours. Jerusalem and the Holy Temple are destroyed, the people are being held captive as slaves in Babylon. Here you will join with some slaves as they are set free to return home and engage in the noble and glorious work of rebuilding the city and the Temple of God. It is during this rebuilding that they make a discovery that brings to light the greatest treasure of a Mason – the long lost Master's Word.

Many historians have traced the earliest origins of the Royal Arch Degree to Ireland, late in the 17th century and in England in 1738. In 1752, ambulatory or military warrants for lodges were introduced. This was instrumental in placing the Royal Arch Degree on a par with the Master Mason Degree. Military lodges were greatly responsible for planting Freemasonry in the Colonies and also gave birth to the use of the Marl and Royal Arch degrees in the "New World." Lodge records show that the Royal Arch Degree was conferred at Fredericksburg No. 4 on December 12, 1753. George Washington was raised [i.e., symbolically resurrected to became a Master Mason] in this lodge a few months prior to this date.

The value of Royal Arch Masonry will be appreciated by all who are exalted to that most sublime degree, particularly by those who are seeking to complete their Masonic education. It reveals the full light of Ancient Craft Masonry, presents it as a complete system in accordance with the original plan and justly entitles you to claim the noble name of Master Mason."*

I don't suppose either the United States of America's first president and Church of England Episcopalian George Washington (1732–1799) or Canada's first Prime Minister, Sir John A. MacDonald (1819–1891), entered Freemasonry for the same reason I did. I was seeking God. I thought that Christians were like sheep – and I didn't want to be a sheep! That's why I didn't attend church to look for God! The

---

* (www.themasonictrowel.com/Articles/apendent_bodies/york/further_light_masonry_royal_arch_
mason.htm)

truth is that I had been put off of Christianity by the Pentecostal televangelist "preachers" who inundated Canadian television at the time. I was afraid of their Christianity. There were numerous televangelist scandals in the late 1980s, so, understandably, I thought "the church" was only after people's minds and money. But a new chapter began in my life when I joined the Chapter of Royal Arch Masonry. It was there that I was confronted by "the stone the builders rejected."

A Dog, a Bird, and a Donkey

J'LL never forget the dog we had when I was growing up. His name was Diamond. He was about the size of a Labrador with a black-and-white, medium-length hair coat. I suppose he was a Labrador retriever/Border collie cross. He was called Diamond on account of a big white diamond formation on the back of his neck. He loved chasing seagulls and would start barking in the air at the mere mention of the word "seagulls"!

In his younger days, he was swift enough to give the rabbits on the hill at the back of Tullichewan in the Vale of Leven a run for their money. I was not impressed with Diamond the time he caught a baby rabbit and had it half eaten by the time I arrived on the scene! Otherwise our regular hill-walking together was great. Every young boy needs a dog!

The strange thing about Diamond was that at one point he had at least three or four groups of people who thought they had some claim to him, viz., the Ewarts on whose farm on the east side of Balloch Diamond had been born, Lynn's Boatyard on the eastern shore of the River Leven at Balloch, a family at the front of Tullichewan, and my family who lived up the back of Tullichewan. Diamond would often go "walkabout" and could be found at various times lodging at any one of these places. Eventually we were accepted as the rightful "owners" of Diamond. However, this didn't stop Diamond from wandering, eventually mostly between our place and Lynn's Boatyard. "Bath time" for Diamond was a swim in the Leven. Like most, if not all dogs, Diamond had a penchant for rolling in smelly dead things. This made it hard sometimes to welcome him home from his travels!

Diamond got along famously with Jock, the young jackdaw* I had found one summer's day while going strawberry picking at Sir Patrick Telfer-Smollet's orchard at his Cameron House estate. Jock was very friendly and all the kids in my class at Levenvale Primary School were suitably impressed by his antics when I was allowed to bring him in one day for Show and Tell. Jock the jackdaw just loved bright shiny objects. This led to a problem. My youngest sister, Mhairi, was about to be born. The big fear was that Jock would peck Mhairi's eyes as she lay in her pram. Taking a 10-year-old's jackdaw from him is like removing one of his limbs! But Jock the jackdaw had to go. There was a nice couple who lived in Caldarvan, a stop on the old and disused railway line to Stirling. Caldarvan is a fair few miles from Tullichewan. I was told I could visit whenever I wanted. I wanted to visit every day. I did manage the trip a few times, walking the many miles alone along the old line through the beautiful countryside. I can still hear the bees buzzing, and I can still taste the juicy raspberries, goose-gogs, and the green ground leaves we called "sourocks" that I found and ate along the way. These all served to keep me filled and happy on the trip.

I can't say I remember ever finding the couple at home whenever I arrived unannounced at their place. Jock was never anywhere in sight either. However, the couple did own a donkey, so my long walks weren't a total waste of time. I fancied myself as a bit of a cowboy. The donkey was my trusty steed. Only once did the donkey ever do anything more than stand in one spot with me astride his back. One day he decided that he would make a bolt for his wooden stall. As he dashed into his stall, I raised my arms and was left dangling from the crossbeam above the entrance. For some reason, the donkey was

---

* A crowlike Eurasian bird (*American Heritage Dictionary*, Dell, 1983).

most annoyed with me and let his displeasure be known with the usual donkey bronchial and asthmatic hee-hawing.

As the weeks and months went by, it was eventually communicated to me that Jock the jackdaw had gone missing and was presumed dead. I remember looking out my parents' bedroom window toward Caldarvan and praying to God with tears – many tears! – for Him to send Jock back to me. Jock never returned. So I fell out with God, and, like a spoiled child holding his breath because he didn't get his own way, remained in a huff with Him.

Christianity and Freemasonry

*A*s a Freemason living in Canada and desiring to learn more about God, I began to notice that some Christians claimed an incompatibility of Christianity with Freemasonry. I sought refuge and solace in a book by Christopher Haffner titled *Workman Unashamed*. In this book, Haffner gives a Masonic "apologetic" from Scripture against anti-Masonic literature.

Being both a new Christian and a new Freemason, I found it somewhat difficult to be a Christian in Masonic circles, but even more so a Mason in Christian circles! However, I found most of the anti-Masonic literature written by Christians to be unconvincing on account of the invariable and obvious lack of knowledge of Masonic ritual and the obvious dependency upon Masonic "exposures" – which tend to be gross distortions and caricatures of lodge activity and Masonic belief. Meanwhile, I continued to study the Scriptures while I studied Freemasonry.

Subsequently, I departed from Freemasonry because I couldn't personally reconcile the fact that, in the interest of lodge "harmony," I was required to leave Jesus outside the door of the lodge on account of the fact that Christians share the lodge with Jews, Muslims,

Hindus, and Buddhists, i.e., other men who do not worship Jesus as God. The final sentence of the following abbreviated quote from the "Aims and Relationships of the Craft," as displayed on the Grand Lodge of Scotland's Website, neatly expresses what my dilemma was as a Mason who was also a Christian:

> In August 1938, the Grand Lodges of England, Ireland, and Scotland each agreed upon and issued a statement identical in terms except that the name of the issuing Grand Lodge appeared throughout. This statement, which was entitled "Aims and Relationships of the Craft," was in the following terms:
> . . .
>
> 3. The first condition of admission into, and membership of, the Order is a belief in the Supreme Being. This is essential and admits of no compromise.
> 4. The Bible, referred to by Freemasons as the Volume of the Sacred Law, is always open in the Lodges. Every candidate is required to take his obligation on that Book, or on the Volume which is held by his particular Creed to impart sanctity to an oath or promise taken upon it.
> . . .
>
> 6. While Scottish Freemasonry inculcates in each of its members the duties of loyalty and citizenship, it reserves to the individual the right to hold his own opinion with regard to public affairs. But neither in any Lodge nor at any time in his capacity as a Freemason is he permitted to discuss or to advance his views on theological or political questions. (*Emphasis mine*, www.grandlodgescotland.com.)

It is clearly seen in the above abbreviated quote that Christianity and the claims of Christ in the "Volume of the Sacred Law" are placed "on the level" and "squared" with other religions! By reading the Bible – which my own lodge had presented me, and encouraged me to read! – I had discovered that the Bible plainly teaches that Jesus Christ is God in the flesh, and therefore must be worshiped as God by all men and angels. But, as a member of the Masonic lodge, I was not permitted to talk about what it says in the Bible that lies open on the altar in the lodge!

And, if I've correctly understood what the Grand Lodges of Scotland etc. are stating in article 6 above, it means that even when not in a lodge at work, if people know me to be a Mason, I'm supposed to mention a disclaimer that any Christian views I have on theology and politics are not the views held by Freemasonry.

The theologian and politician Abraham Kuyper (1837–1920), Prime Minister of the Netherlands (1901–1905), sums up the dilemma for every Christian Mason when he says, "In the total expanse of human life there is not a single square inch of which the Christ, who alone is sovereign, does not declare, 'That is mine!'" But what are the views held and taught by Blue Lodge Masonry? That other religions stand equal to Christianity! Thus Masonry wrongly teaches an equal ultimacy between Christianity and other religions, or, to put it another way, Masonry teaches that the true and living God (who has revealed Himself in Jesus Christ) is equal to false gods! Talk about having one foot on the boat and the other on the pier when the boat is leaving!

One group of American Masons points to something of the tension I was feeling as I tried to be a good Mason and a Christian obedient to Christ:

> Masonry acknowledges the existence of God. No atheist can become a Mason. Prayer is an important part of the Masonic ritual. Masonic vows are taken in the name of God, but Masonry never tries to tell a person how he should think about God, or how he should worship God, or why he should believe. We offer no plan of salvation. We teach that man should live a good life, not because that alone will earn him entrance into heaven, but because anything else is destructive, both to himself and to those around him. It is good to be good. As to whether a man can be a Mason and a Christian, the best answer is that most [of] us are. There are many Free Masons who belong to other faiths, including Judaism, Islam, Hinduism, and Buddhism, but the majority in America are Christian. And we number many, many

ministers of many different denominations. As Dr. Norman Vincent Peale, an active Freemason himself, once remarked: "Masonry encourages men to be good and that can never conflict with Christianity." *

The answer to the question as to whether a Christian ought to be a Mason I'll leave to the reader to decide, but a wonderful thing indeed it would be if all Freemasons were Christians! That would certainly have solved my dilemma. But the truth is that Judaists, Islamists, and Buddhists share the same lodges with Christians. Thus the Masonic lodge is obviously not designed to be exclusive to the Christian Faith. That was where my problem lay! I had no personal grudge against Judaists, Islamists, Hindus, or Buddhists, but, because of Masonic design, if I were to be obedient to Masonic teaching, I could not bring Jesus Christ with me into my lodge.

It also ought to be noted that the Dr. Norman Vincent Peale (1898–1993) mentioned above was an American Methodist minister ordained in 1922. He joined the Reformed Church in America in 1932. He is perhaps best known for his book *The Power of Positive Thinking* (1952) in which, for all his mingling with Calvinism and Calvinists, he betrays an obvious liberal or modernistic influence by his blending psychotherapy with Christianity, by which I mean the teachings of the Bible. *Sola Scriptura* means "Scripture Alone" and expresses the Reformation teaching of the authority and sufficiency of the Scriptures by which all matters of faith and practice may be settled. According to this teaching, only that which the Bible deems to be good is good. Therefore, whatever doesn't line up with Scripture is deception.

---

* www.masonic-network.com/green.html

Quatuor Coronati

$\mathscr{P}$ROF. Wallace McLeod (a Mason in Toronto) was lamenting a couple of articles that appeared in the December 1986 *Presbyterian Record* (a publication of the Presbyterian Church in Canada). In this issue, Prof. McLeod stated, "There were two attacks on Freemasonry, largely on the grounds that it is a non-Christian religion." A spirited correspondence ensued over the next six months. Among the points at issue was the appellation "the Great Architect of the Universe." One of the original contributors had said that "it makes God seem like an abstract being," while another stated that this was the name of the "false god that Masons worship at their altar."

Prof. McLeod responded by firing back a very interesting letter that was eventually published in the May 1987 edition of the *The Presbyterian Record*. It ran, in part, as follows:

> Actually this phrase ["the Great Architect of the Universe"] entered Freemasonry by way of the first Book of Constitutions, printed in 1723. The compiler was Revd. Dr. James Anderson, a graduate of Aberdeen University, and minister of the Scotch Presbyterian Church in Swallow Street, Piccadilly, London, from 1710 to 1734. He did not invent the phrase but took it over from John Calvin, who uses it, for example, in his Commentary on Psalm 19; the heavens "were wonderfully founded by the Great Architect" (*ab opifice praestantissimo*); again, according to the same paragraph, "when once we recognize God as the Architect of the Universe (*mundi opificem*), we are bound to marvel at his Wisdom, Strength, and Goodness." In fact, Calvin repeatedly calls God "the Architect of the Universe" and refers to his works in nature as "Architecture of the Universe" ten times in the *Institutes of the Christian Religion* alone. I may be missing something, but it seems to me bizarre that writers in the national publication of the Presbyterian Church in Canada should suddenly find fault with words that have been part of Calvinism for four centuries. (*Ars Quatuor Coronatorum: Transactions of Quatuor Coronati Lodge No. 2076*, Vol. 101 for the year 1988, 146–147.)

I was able to find only one instance in Calvin's *Institutes of the Christian Religion* where Calvin refers to God as "Architect of the Universe," (i.e., Beverage Translation, Book 1:5:4). While I was unable to find the other references to "Architecture of the Universe," I did find "artificer of the universe" a couple of times in the Battles translation of Calvin's *Institutes*. Nevertheless, as can be seen, Calvin does indeed refer once to God as the "Architect of the Universe" in his *Institutes!* It was careless Christians with slip-shod research of Freemasonry (or lack thereof) that kept me in Freemasonry and away from attending church for so long! In hindsight, the way I see it, Christianity, like Freemasonry, has its share of people inside and outside who, though well-meaning, hold distorted views of each.

I joined The Correspondence Circle of Quatuor Coronati (the Masonic Research Lodge) to find out what Freemasonry was all about. Quatuor Coronati presents research papers on Masonry and all things related for its brethren to critique.

The Architect of the Universe

*M*y personal search for God was on account of the things He had made. I could see that there was an order to creation simply by observing the night sky. It seemed to me that the Big Bang should have brought chaos, not order. And who made the material that supposedly "big banged"? Clearly the heavens are of a grand design. Clearly they are the handiwork of a great architect. I couldn't deny it. And why should I deny it? Thus, I wanted to know the One who made the stars.

King David, the sweet psalmist of Israel, wrote the following words by inspiration of the Holy Spirit: "The heavens declare the glory of God; and the firmament shows His handiwork" (Ps. 19:1). John Calvin, in the following comment on this verse, sums up where I was in my relationship with God when I entered Freemasonry (note also that Calvin refers to God here as the supreme Architect):

> David shows how it is that the heavens proclaim to us the glory of God, namely, by openly bearing testimony that they have not been put together by chance, but were wonderfully created by the supreme Architect. When we behold the heavens, we cannot but be elevated by the contemplation of them to Him who is their great Creator; and the beautiful arrangement and wonderful variety which distinguish the courses and station of the heavenly bodies, together with the beauty and splendor which are manifest in them, cannot but furnish us with an evident proof of His providence. Scripture, indeed, makes known to us the time and manner of the creation, but the heavens themselves, although God should say nothing on the subject, proclaim loudly and distinctly enough that they have been fashioned by His hands: and this of itself abundantly suffices to bear testimony to men of His glory. As soon as we acknowledge God to be the supreme Architect who has erected the beauteous fabric of the universe, our minds must necessarily be ravished with wonder at His infinite goodness, wisdom, and power.
>
> (Calvin, *Commentaries: Joshua and the Psalms.* Grand Rapids: Associated Publishers & Authors, Inc.)

Something To Crow About

$\mathcal{I}$ WAS about 12 or 13 when I found a baby crow in the Croftamie woods while out walking with one of my Vale of Leven Academy schoolmates who lived out that way. I called the little crow Squawk and took him home to Tullichewan with me. Squawk was every bit as playful as Jock the jackdaw had been two or three years earlier. One time we had pitched the old tent in the backyard to give it a bit of an airing. Squawk would land on the ridge of the tent with a small stone in his beak. He would release it and watch it roll down the sloped incline of the tent's roof. He was heard "muttering" and "chuckling" as he kept on repeating this exercise.

Mind you, Diamond the dog wasn't too impressed with Squawk, who, after he had matured and was able to fly, would land on Diamond's back, hold on to his collar so that he wouldn't be thrown off, and peck the back of Diamond's head real hard. Diamond would run for his life whenever this happened!

It was a real thrill for me taking the two of them for walks "up the hill" into the woods behind Tullichewan. Squawk would always come to me when called. In fact, it was really difficult for me to get to school in the morning without Squawk seeing me. He always wanted to go everywhere with me. One time I was sitting on the top deck of a double-decker bus on my way to school when someone said, "Look, there's a crow flying beside the window of the bus!" Rats! He had spotted me on the bus! I had to get off and take Squawk home. That wasn't the only day I was late for school!

One day in the school library I spotted a book with an interesting title: "Neil and His Jackdaw." Apparently the female half of the couple who had been given Jock the jackdaw had written a children's book loosely based on me and my jackdaw! At the time, for some strange reason, I wasn't that impressed about there being a book based on Jock and me, though I wish I had that book now!

Three in One

THE first three degrees of Masonry (i.e., the degrees of the Blue Lodge) refer to the Creator as the "Great Architect of the Universe," the "Grand Geometrician," and the "Most High," respectively.

The Bible is referred to and quoted from in the various lectures of these three degrees. Therefore, God is also spoken of as "Lord," "the LORD," "Creator," and, of course, "God." Thus, without a doubt, it is the God who has revealed Himself in the sixty-six books of the Bible, in both the Old and New Testaments, who is being spoken of in Blue Lodge Freemasonry.

Indeed, the opening verses of the Bible are verbally repeated early on in one of the degrees. As one would expect, these verses fit perfectly with the Triune nature of God, stating, "In the beginning God created the heaven and the earth. And the earth was without form, and void; and darkness was upon the face of the deep. And the Spirit of God moved upon the face of the waters. And God said, Let there be light: and there was light" (Gen. 1:1–3, KJV). The Bible throughout makes it very clear that the Creator God is Father, Son, and Holy Spirit (see Matt. 28:18; 2 Cor. 13:14).

The Triune God also is spoken of as "the Father," "the Word," and "the Holy Ghost" or "Spirit" (1 John 5:7, KJV; Matt. 3:16–17; Mark 1:10–11; Luke 3:22; John 1:1; Rev. 19:13). Thus, the Father, the Word, and the Spirit are seen to be together in the beginning: The Father, with creative intent, spoke the Word, and the Spirit brought creation into being. We see this initial act of creation reflected somewhat in the temple-building actions of the threesome, viz., King Solomon; Hiram, king of Tyre; and Hiram the master craftsman. Solomon made the request; Hiram, king of Tyre complied. And the other Hiram, the master craftsman, shaped the material into the Temple at Jerusalem.

Also, regarding the Triune nature of God, Genesis was originally written in Hebrew, which, unlike English, has singular, dual, and plural words. Thus Genesis 1:1 says in effect: "In the beginning God [i.e., Elohim, who is a plurality of at least three Persons] created [singular, as in "He" created] the heavens and the earth." Indeed Deuteronomy, the fifth Book of Moses, testifies to the singularity and plurality of God where it states: "Hear, O Israel: The LORD our God, the LORD is one!" (Deut. 6:4).

English Bibles tend to substitute the word "LORD" for the Hebrew tetragrammaton usually represented by the equivalent English letters

YHWH. We derive the word JeHoVaH or YeHoWaH from YHWH. Therefore, Deuteronomy 6:4b actually reads: "Jehovah our God, [i.e., our plurality of Persons] is one Jehovah." Even the word "YHWH" arguably is derived from Hebrew verbs for the three tenses of time: Je (future), Ho (present), Vah (past), thus signifying that God is the Eternal One. English Bibles also tend to use the word "Lord" (lower case letters) to translate the Hebrew word "Adonai," which means Lord, as in Master.

That God is Triune is borne out in a verse that deals with God creating man: "Then God said, 'Let *Us* make man in *Our* image, according to *Our* likeness;…' So God created man in His own image; in the image of God He created him; male and female He created them" (Gen. 1:26–27, *emphasis mine*).

I have heard many ingenious explanations put forth about the words "Us" and "Our" in this verse by non-Christians and, indeed, anyone who denies that God is the Triune Father, Son, and Holy Spirit. But that's their problem. My problem was that I wanted to know the Creator God personally. I wanted to have a personal relationship with Almighty God. I wanted to be able to relate to Him.

Yes, God is the Great Architect of the Universe. Yes, He is the Grand Geometrician. Yes, He is the Most High God. But I wondered if it was possible to have a *relationship* with Him as, for example, did King David when he wrote: "The LORD said to my Lord, sit at My right hand till I make Your enemies Your footstool" (Psalm 110:1).

> Glory be to God the Father,
> Glory be to God the Son,
> Glory be to God the Spirit,
> Great Jehovah, Three in One!
> Glory, glory,
> While eternal ages run.
>
> — Horatius Bonar (1808–1889)
> Hymn 7, RCH

Lost in Space

*I*N the Blue Lodge degrees, God is merely acknowledged in a generic sort of way. After the third and final Blue Lodge degree (the Master Mason), I was left with the clear sense that a piece of the "God-puzzle" was still very much missing. Indeed, the three degrees are designed in such a way as to have the Master Mason seek further knowledge. The Second Degree, in particular, certainly encourages the Mason to study the "liberal arts and sciences." Theology is a science. Therefore, I continued to study the revealed will of God to man, i.e., the Holy Bible.

I had been corresponding from Canada with Fearghas, my eldest brother living in Scotland. In a letter I told him that I was "seeking" God. He had already been a Christian for many years by this time. Fearghas is an art teacher. I remembered one of his paintings in particular. My parents had hung it on one of the walls of their bedroom. The painting was done in the 1960s or perhaps the early '70s. It depicted a man in a spacesuit floating in space. Somehow his attachment cord had come loose from his spaceship. He was lost in space! Scary thought.

In his letters to me, my brother gave me wonderful advice about how to find God. However, in particular, a single verse – in fact, it was half of a verse of Scripture – that he had quoted stuck in my mind, lodged in my heart, and repeated itself over and over: "Jesus said to him, 'I am the way, the truth, and the life. *No one comes to the Father except through Me.*'" (John 14:6, *emphasis mine*). I remember thinking to myself, Who does Jesus think He is? I sat in my basement on Molson Street, in North Kildonan, Manitoba, pondering the deeper things of life. Is life really summed-up in the bumper-sticker slogan, "The one who dies with the most toys wins"? Surely there is something more, more than materialism. Does one just live for a bit and then die? Is there no real and deeper meaning to it all, no purpose? The "brain imbalance" of my youth came back to haunt me! The evolutionist in me was telling me that "life" was simply all about the propagation of the human species! Carl Sagan – whom I had watched in his television series "Cosmos" – like some background radiation hum in the universe, was reciting, as it were, the prayer-mantra of the evolutionist in my one ear, "this is all there is, this is all there was, and this is all there ever will be," while in my other ear I could hear the words, "No one comes to the Father except through Me."

As I deeply contemplated life and God I began to feel more and more like the spaceman in my brother's painting: Drifting. Isolated. Cold. Lonely. So very cold and lonely!

After going through the three Blue Lodge degrees, I had further gone through the four other degrees of the Chapter of the Royal Arch. These further four degrees had compelled me to a deeper study of God's Word on account of their use of the Scriptures in their rituals and lectures. Indeed, one of the degrees refers to the finding of the Gospel According to John, which Gospel begins with the very verse I had been disputing over with the so called Jehovah's Witnesses: "In the beginning was the Word, and the Word was *with* God, and the Word *was* God" (John 1:1, *emphasis mine*). There is an obvious connection between this verse and the opening verses of the Bible in Genesis. The verses directly following go on to say: "The same [He] was in the beginning *with* God. All things *were made by Him*; and without Him was not anything made that was made. In Him was life; and the life was the light of men. And the light shineth in darkness; and the darkness comprehended it not" (John 1:2-5, KJV, *emphasis mine*).

How could Jesus *be* God and also be *with* God? I was soon to discover that He could be both God and with God in the same way that the LORD speaks to king David's Lord in Psalm 110:1. David's "Lord" was Christ the eternal Son of God before His incarnation. For Jesus Christ is God the Second Person in the Trinity become also flesh: "And the Word was made flesh, and dwelt among us, (and we beheld His glory, the glory as of the only begotten of the Father,) full of grace and truth" (John 1:14, KJV).

Lonely Journey

WHILE going through my conversion, I was wrestling with issues such as the tension between man's free will and the sovereignty of God. I recall my brother Fearghas saying that these things meet in eternity, kind of like parallel railroad tracks meeting in the far-off horizon. The consistent Calvinist, as I was to learn, holds man's responsibility and God's sovereignty in an equal and balanced tension. While God is 100 percent sovereign, He holds man 100 percent responsible for his actions. It's kind of like the Bible: 100 percent of it is written by God while 100 percent is written by men. But somehow this doesn't add up to 200 percent, only 100 percent! Such is the mystery of God's sovereignty and man's responsibility – it can't be worked out with a simple mathematical, theological, or any other sort of equation. Regardless, going through the whole conversion experience was a lonely time for me. I wrote:

Lonesome Train

I felt at the wicket from the price of the ticket
    I was witness to a serious crime!
I turned and shook my head
    as the Stationmaster said,
"Good grief! The train is on time!"

Is it predestination
    when your train leaves the station
    and journeys to someplace new?
Or is it just a bore when you've seen it all before
    like some permanent déjà vu?
Lonesome train, take me away!

Is it providence or fate
    when you enter through the gate
    to find your train standing on the wrong track?
Does your heart skip a beat when you notice
    that your seat has got your name
    printed on a gold plaque?

With a teardrop in your eye you just smile
  and wave goodbye,
    you're trying to escape from your mind.
But on the rack above your head,
  there's a suitcase full of dread.
You packed the things
  you should have left behind.
Lonesome train, take me away!

You've got to travel fast to escape a shady past
  but the present always hangs around.
The future's always near, but it never gets that clear
  when you don't know where your train is bound.
You won't clean out your mind,
  you're afraid you're going to find
    some thought that's going to cause you pain.

But the world still passes by
  out of the corner of your eye
    when you sit aboard that lonesome train.
Lonesome train, take me away
  to a bright new day.
It's a bright new day.

The Stone the Builders Rejected

To be converted by the sovereign God is to experience a life and worldview "rebuilding" process. It is a being set free from a former slavery. Figuratively speaking, it is a returning to Eden. It is being raised from the dead. It is to go from darkness to light.

Whereas Blue Lodge has to do with building Solomon's Temple, Red Lodge (or at least the Chapter of Royal Arch aspect of Red Lodge) has to do with rebuilding the Temple.

The Royal Arch Degree is the capstone of Ancient Craft Masonry and Masonic Symbolism. It is described as "the root and marrow of Freemasonry." It is the complete story of Jewish History during some of its darkest hours. Jerusalem and the Holy Temple are destroyed, the people of Israel are being held captive as slaves in Babylon. Here you will join with some of the captives as they are set free to return home and engage in the noble and glorious work of rebuilding the city and the Temple of God. It is during this rebuilding that they discover a crypt, and the value of the resulting discoveries to the Craft are immeasurable, for it brings to light the greatest treasure of a Mason – the long lost Master's Word.*

If the destroyed Temple represents Paradise Lost, i.e., fallen man ejected from the Garden of Eden for breaking the covenant by disobeying God by eating the forbidden fruit, then the rebuilding of the Temple must represent Paradise Regained, i.e., re-entering the Garden. The veil in the Temple separating the Holy of Holies, where God was said to dwell between the cherubim on the Ark of the Covenant, had cherubim and palm trees woven into it. The veil represented the barrier of sin separating fallen man from Holy God, reminiscent of the cherubim and the turning flaming sword at the gate of the Garden of Eden.

The destroyed relationship between man and God needed to be rebuilt. The LORD God walked with man before man disobeyed Him in the Garden. After the Fall and the time of Moses who received the Law, God met once a year with the High Priest (who was the representative of the people) – but not without the accompaniment of the shed blood of bulls and goats as a "sin covering" and which was sprinkled on the Mercy Seat (the lid of the Ark of the Covenant), to atone for the people's wrongdoings. The destroyed Temple also represented man's heart, i.e., his innermost being, the place where man meets God – sin-blackened, destroyed.

In one of the Royal Arch degrees, it is mentioned that a peculiarly shaped stone is found among the ruins and rubble of the Temple

---

* www.royalarchmasonalberta.com/index.php/welcome/about-us.

that had been destroyed. And that this peculiar stone is the stone the builders rejected. I could see that this stone clearly represented Jesus Christ who, when He had chased the moneylenders from His Father's house (the Temple), had said: "'Destroy this temple, and in three days I will raise it up.' Then the Jews said, 'It has taken forty-six years to build this temple, and You will raise it up in three days?' But He was speaking of the temple of His body. Therefore, when He had risen from the dead, His disciples remembered that He had said this to them; and they believed the Scripture and the word which Jesus had said" (John 2:19–22).

In the Chapter of Royal Arch, its members are likened to the destroyed Temple being rebuilt and even the stones used in that rebuilding. But more importantly, not only is Jesus Christ likened to the Temple that had been destroyed (crucified) and rebuilt again (resurrected), but He is also called "the stone the builders rejected" who becomes the "chief cornerstone" or the stone that is the "head of the corner" (1 Pet. 2:6–7).

The "builders" were those Jews who kept rejecting Jesus as Messiah (i.e., the Christ or the Anointed of God). These are the same who had the Romans crucify Him on trumped up charges. Thus Jesus became the stone the builders rejected and the destroyed Temple of God – exactly what the earthly Temple had symbolized.

In the Royal Arch ritual, the stone the builders rejected is said to have been discarded among the rubble of the destroyed Temple. This stone is called a "keystone." What was the peculiar characteristic of this stone? It was neither oblong nor square, and is referenced as the keystone or copestone (i.e., the stone forming a coping, or the "finishing touch"). According to Masonic legends, the builders of the Temple of Solomon became bewildered when they received this particular stone, and since it was neither oblong nor square as they were used to receiving, they subsequently threw it aside. They later found that this stone was very necessary and important, and that it was to become the head of the corner (Matt. 21:42; Mark 12:10; see also *The Bible and King Solomon's Temple in Masonry* by John Wesley Kelchner).

In the Book of Zechariah it is recorded that Zerubbabel was given the task of rebuilding the original destroyed Temple. However, though literal and real, the rebuilding of the Temple is simply a picture of something equally real, but spiritual: "This is the word of the LORD to Zerubbabel: 'Not by might nor by power, but by My Spirit,' says the LORD of hosts. 'Who are you, O great mountain? Before Zerubbabel you shall become a plain! And he shall bring forth the capstone with shouts of "Grace! Grace to it!"'" (Zech. 4:6–7).

Jesus Christ is the great archetype of the capstone. He was raised from the dead by the power of the Spirit (Rom. 1:4; Heb. 9:14; 1 Pet. 3:18). In the grand scheme of things, Jesus Christ is both the cornerstone and the capstone of the New Creation. Under the sovereign and inscrutable God, the old creation was destroyed by sin but is now resurrected and is progressively being renewed, by the Spirit of the Father and the Son, on account of Jesus' resurrection.

Jesus Christ is the Mediator between God and men. He is both God and Man in one Divine Person forever. By His two natures, the Divine and the human united, Jesus Christ is God and Man – who were once at war with each other – now reconciled forever. He is the new Temple of God – the place where God dwells: "For in Him [Jesus Christ] dwells all the fullness of Godhead bodily" (Col. 2:9). Christ by His Spirit indwells His people, i.e., all those whom God converts by His Word and Spirit. These are progressively being transformed into the image of Jesus Christ the perfect Man.

> Christ be with me, Christ within me,
> Christ behind me, Christ before me,
> Christ beside me, Christ to win me,
> Christ to comfort and restore me,
> Christ beneath me, Christ above me,
> Christ in quiet, Christ in danger,
> Christ in hearts of all that love me,
> Christ in mouth of friend and stranger.
>
> – St. Patrick (372–466)
> Version by Cecil Frances
> Alexander (1818–95)
> Hymn 506, RCH

The Ineffable Name

*T*HE remarkable thing that took place in my life was that, on account of what I went through and saw acted out in the Royal Arch, I could see clearly that Jesus Christ was indeed Jehovah in the flesh, i.e., the true stone the builders rejected – the stone over which the builders were stumbling. I could see clearly that the Bible teaches that by rejecting Jesus, those Jews who refused to believe Jesus was the Messiah (promised throughout the Old Testament Scriptures) were rejecting the living and true God!

It was through the Royal Arch's reference to arches that I was led to see that the stone the builders rejected was indeed Jehovah – clearly demonstrated in the Bible to be also Jesus Christ the Son of God. I was helped along to this conclusion by the well-known Mason, Harry Carr in his book *Harry Carr's World of Freemasonry* wherein writes Carr:

> THE INEFFABLE NAME. The Oxford English Dictionary gives two sets of definitions for the word "ineffable" that are applicable in a Masonic context:
>
> 1. That cannot be expressed or described in language; too great for words; transcending expression; unspeakable, inexpressible.
>
> 2. That must not be uttered; not to be disclosed or made known (obsolete).
>
> The Name is the Tetragrammaton, the word of four Hebrew letters. Yod, Hé, Vav, Hé, usually rendered Y H W H or J H V H and it is pronounced (by those permitted to do so) as Yahweh or Jehovah. Even within the range of definitions quoted above, "the Name" has enormous implications since it was supposed to express, within itself, those attributes of God which are beyond verbal expression, too great for words. For all whose faith is bound up in the VSL (Old and New Testaments)* "The Name" always had the mysterious

---

* Harry Carr is referring to the standard King James Version Bible! (VSL [or VOSL] = Volume of the Sacred Law.)

quality of representing an idea of the Deity beyond human powers of description. For the Jews, however, "the Name" is ineffable in a still wider sense because it is forbidden to be uttered – even in prayer – except by the Priests in the course of the Priestly benediction. For all others of the Ancient Faith, when "the Name" appears in the Prayer Book or in Holy Writ, a substitute word is used and the ineffable name is read as Adonai (The Lord).... There can be no doubt, however, that the Ineffable Name was one of the links between the earlier Craft degrees [i.e., Blue Lodge] and the Royal Arch. (Revised Edition, 1985, 363)

The Blue Lodge degrees used a substitute word for "the Name," therefore, it wasn't until I had gone through the Red Lodge degrees that the "key" was given to me for understanding the God of Masonry. And in no uncertain terms, the Red Lodge equates the "ineffable name" (i.e., YHWH) with Jesus, "the stone the builders rejected." This is alluded to in a portion of an earlier quote (used above and again here) which, while extolling the virtues of the Royal Arch, says:

> Here you will join with some slaves as they are set free to return home and engage in the noble and glorious work of rebuilding the city and the Temple of God. It is during this rebuilding that they make a discovery that brings to light the greatest treasure of a Mason – the long lost Master's Word.*

The "slaves returning home" is alluding to the time the people of God were released after their seventy-years of Babylonian captivity and returned to rebuild Jerusalem and the Temple. King Nebuchadnezzar had destroyed Solomon's Temple and had carted off to hold in captivity the important people of Israel, circa 586 B.C. Zerubbabel is the prominent figure in the rebuilding of the Temple after the return of the Israelites. As already mentioned, the final degree in the Chapter of the Royal Arch refers to a strangely shaped stone supposedly found among the rubble of the destroyed Temple of Solomon.

---

* www.royalarchmasonalberta.com/index.php/welcome/about-us.

I had been taught in the Blue Lodge that Masonry is synonymous with Geometry. Therefore, when the stone the builders rejected was referred to as a keystone that holds an archway together I started studying the shapes of keystones. And Lo! and Behold! Did the Hebrew letters in the Tetragrammaton (YHWH) when viewed in terms of their numerical equivalents, not present the shape of a trapezoid otherwise known as a keystone? Y = Yod, the tenth (10) letter in the Hebrew alphabet; H = Hé, the fifth (5); W = Vav, the sixth letter (6); and H = again Hé, the fifth (5). Jesus was the keystone and the keystone was JeHoVaH! Find a piece of paper and draw lines forming a box shape with the dimensions 10 x 5 x 6 x 5 (use millimetres or inches) and the shape of a keystone will appear. This was astounding to me!

If you remove the keystone from an arch, the arch falls down. My personal darkness turned to light when I realized the reality that Jesus Christ is – in every way – the keystone that holds the entire creation together (see Col. 1:17). Christ is the "missing link"!

God's Mercy

Is there an analogical relationship between what happened to Solomon's Temple, the great Deluge in Noah's day, and what happened to the Garden of Eden? Solomon's Temple was eventually sacked and destroyed by Nebuchadnezzar who took Israel into captivity in 586 B.C. Thus, though the homeland of the Israelites was destroyed, the people themselves were preserved. This illustrates both the justice and the mercy of God. So does the great Flood in Noah's day.

Was the Garden buried under a pile of mud and debris in the global flood of God's judgment upon the wickedness of mankind in Noah's day? Well, if the building and rebuilding of Solomon's Temple symbolizes anything, surely it's the "mercy of God." Scripture tells us

He restores the years the locust has eaten (Joel 2:25), and that even in His wrath He remembers mercy (Hab. 3:2). Thus, the great wooden ship we call Noah's Ark was, essentially, a floating Garden of Eden.

> Out of the ground the LORD God (i.e., Jehovah Elohim) formed every beast of the field and every bird of the air, and brought them to Adam to see what he would call them. (Genesis 2:19)
>
> The LORD God said to Noah, "Make yourself an ark of gopherwood; make rooms in the ark, and cover it inside and outside with pitch. And this is how you shall make it: The length of the ark shall be three hundred cubits, its width fifty cubits, and its height thirty cubits. You shall make a window for the ark, and you shall finish it to a cubit from above; and set the door of the ark in its side. You shall make it with lower, second, and third decks. And behold, I Myself am bringing floodwaters on the earth, to destroy from under heaven all flesh in which is the breath of life; everything that is on the earth shall die. But I will establish My covenant with you; and you shall go into the ark – you, your sons, your wife, and your son's wives with you.... Of the birds after their kind, of animals after their kind, and of every creeping thing of the earth after its kind, two of every kind will come to you to keep them alive. And you shall take for yourself of all food that is eaten, and you shall gather it to yourself; and it shall be food for you and for them." (Genesis 6:14–21)

The ark wasn't designed to win the America's Cup; it didn't need to get from Sydney to Hobart in record time. It only needed to stay afloat. Like Solomon's Temple, it contained three decks (or stories). Noah, sawing logs to build the great wooden ark, was a continuation of the Cultural Mandate given to man in the Garden of Eden: "Then God said, 'Let Us make man in Our image, according to Our likeness; let them have dominion over the fish of the sea, over the birds of the air, and over the cattle, over all the earth and over every creeping thing that creeps on the earth'" (Gen. 1:26). Indeed, the Cultural Mandate was reissued to Noah and his family upon their exiting the ark (Gen. 9:1–7).

Like Noah, King Solomon, too, sawed logs. He also was in the business of shipbuilding. "King Solomon also built a fleet of ships at Ezion Geber, which is near Elath on the shore of the Red Sea, in the land of Edom. Then Hiram sent his servants with the fleet, seamen who knew the sea, to work with the servants of Solomon.... Once every three years the merchant ships came bringing gold, silver, ivory, apes, and monkeys" (1 Kings 9:26–27; 10:22).

The Cultural Mandate began for man when the LORD God placed Adam in the garden He had made to tend and keep it. Ever since then, this mandate is being fulfilled even from the cutting down of trees to the building of ships, to the cultivation of plants and animals, and the crafting of gold, silver, and the other ores and precious stones mined from the ground. The making of musical instruments and the singing of praise are also included in the Cultural Mandate. Indeed, all pursuits of mankind are cultural.

Like the Garden of Eden and Noah's Ark, Solomon's Temple was full of birds, animals, plants, and trees. For as Noah made animal sacrifices to God after he came out of the Ark (Gen. 8:20), as did man when he came out of the Garden (Gen. 4:4), so were animal sacrifices begun at the completion of Solomon's Temple. "Then the king and all the people offered sacrifices before the LORD. King Solomon offered a sacrifice of twenty-two thousand bulls and one hundred and twenty thousand sheep. So the king and all the people dedicated the house of God. And the priests attended to their services; the Levites also with instruments of the music of the LORD, which King David had made to praise the LORD, saying, 'For His mercy endures forever,' whenever David offered praise by their ministry. The priests sounded trumpets opposite them, while all Israel stood" (2 Chron. 7:4–6).

What is the significance of animal sacrifice? What is its connection with the Garden of God? Does it have something to do with the expulsion of Adam and Eve from the Garden after they had disobeyed God? Does there need to be a sacrifice before we can draw near to God, before we will be welcomed into Paradise? Adam and Eve covered their shame with leaves, yet the LORD God saw fit to make a more acceptable covering when He made them "garments of skin" (see Gen. 3:21). Was God showing the two that shed blood is the only acceptable covering for sin? I believe we see something of the mercy of God in Biblical sacrifice. All birds and animals belong to Him and He says, "For every beast of the forest is Mine, and the cattle on a thousand hills. I know all the birds of the mountains, and the wild beasts of the field are Mine. If I were hungry, I would not tell you; for the world is Mine, and all its fullness. Will I eat the flesh of bulls, or drink the blood of goats? Offer to God thanksgiving, and pay your vows to the Most High. Call upon Me in the day of trouble; I will deliver you, and you shall glorify Me" (Ps. 50:10–15).

The Paradise Garden of Eden is safe with God. It is Heaven – the dwelling place of God (Rev. 2:7; 22:2,14). For Jesus, the great High Priest, as He was offering up Himself to God as THE sacrifice (to which all Old Testament animal sacrifices pointed) said to the repentant thief on the cross next to Him, "Assuredly, I say to you, today you will be with Me *in Paradise*" (Luke 23:43, *emphasis mine*).

If the Paradise Garden of Eden was on a mountain, i.e., "the holy mountain of God" (e.g., Ezek. 28:13–14 together with Rev. 4:1–6), then it makes perfect sense that the "floating Eden" (i.e., Noah's ark) should come to rest on a mountain, and that Solomon's Temple should be built upon a mountain. Jesus Christ is "a stone cut without hands," from a mountain, which stone itself "became a great mountain that filled the whole earth" (Dan. 2:34-35b, 44; Ps. 118:22; Isa. 8:13-15; Zech. 4:6-9; Matt. 21:42; Mark 12:10-11; Luke 20:17-18; Acts 4:11; Eph. 2:20-22; 1 Pet. 2:4-8).

Thus some future day, and by a gradual growth and progression, the Garden of Eden, the Ark of Salvation, the Temple of God, the Heavenly Paradise (i.e., Christ and His Kingdom of Grace and Peace), will cover the earth as the waters of God's judgment covered the earth in Noah's day. Then "the wolf also shall dwell with the lamb, the leopard shall lie down with the young goat, the calf and the young lion and the fatling together; and a little child shall lead them. The cow and the bear shall graze; their young ones shall lie down together; and the lion shall eat straw like the ox. The nursing child shall play by the cobra's hole, and the weaned child shall put his hand in the viper's den. They shall not hurt nor destroy in all My holy mountain, for the earth shall be full of the knowledge of the LORD as the waters cover the sea" (Isa. 11:6–9).

Armchair Conversion

*N*OT everyone is converted to Christianity the same way as the Pharisee Saul of Tarsus on the road to Damascus. Saul, of course, became Paul the Apostle of Jesus Christ. Indeed some children grow up in Christian homes never knowing the moment of their conversion, knowing only that they have always loved Jesus and have always trusted in Him alone for salvation. In some ways I envy those Christians.

My own conversion was climactic. Like a stuck needle on an old broken record, I was trying to come to grips with Jesus saying, "I am the way, the truth, and the life. No one comes to the Father except through Me" (John 14:6). I thought this exclusivity was very arrogant. I remember sitting in my armchair contemplating these words, and wondering who this Jesus thought He was! The "stone the builders rejected" of the Bible (and of the Chapter of the Royal Arch teaching) was about to really sink into and permanently lodge in my heart.

My brother Fearghas' painting of the spaceman lost in space became how I felt. He had become detached from the mother ship – I was lost in space. The millions of stars were twinkling in the black night sky. I was surrounded by people at work and had my family at home. I played soccer. I had a busy social life. I attended Masonic meetings, but like the drifting spaceman, I began to feel so lonely and detached in the universe. Still, in my heart I pondered the things I had learned about God as I sat in my armchair.

I began to call out to God audibly: "I want to know You!" I had come to the stage in my philosophical travels of being unable to prove to myself whether I was awake or dreaming. It's a terribly terrifying place to be, not knowing if I was dreaming that reality is real, or worse, whether I was part of someone else's dream! How does anyone know if they really exist? How are we to measure reality? Perhaps I was really in a coma lying on a hospital bed somewhere.

Is truth a subjective thing? If it is, then, am I the measure of reality? Am I the centre of the universe? Does the universe cabalistically emanate from me as its centre? (I had delved into cabalism as I fossicked* around in the dusty tomes of Masonic literature in Masonic libraries.)

For there to be objective truth there would need to be a Supreme Being Who had revealed His will to man. Otherwise one man's opinion is as valid as any other man's contradiction.

I believed in a Supreme Being, but who was He? I continued to cry out to Him. And as I did so, I listened in my heart for the answer. But all that I could hear was Jesus saying *I am the way, the truth, and the life. No one comes to the Father except through Me.* I would reply to Him, "Get out of my way. I am looking for God!" And again I would cry out to God. And again Jesus would say, *No one comes to the Father except through Me.* Around and around we would go.

Sitting alone in that armchair I became, in my mind, the spaceman. The severed umbilical cord slowly flapped in the solar wind. The stars in the dark sky continued silently blinking. I began to gasp for air. I felt weak. I gasped for God, for life! "I want to know You, God!" *No one comes to the Father except through Me* was the singular reply. "But I'm looking for God!"

Then it happened. The lights went out in my mind. Not one twinkling star in the black expanse of the universe – only utter darkness! Horror and great darkness fell upon me! Like a fish in a net, or deep in the dark hold of the icy bowels of a fisherman's boat, I feebly gasped for air! "I want to know God!" My cry was very feeble now. Again the words of Jesus entered my mind: *I am the way, the truth, and the life. No one comes to the Father except through Me.*

Tears began to stream down my face when at last I realized who

---

* Australian: Mining term; to rummage about in search of valuables.

Jesus is. He is God! How stupid of me! I had seen it over and over in the Bible, yet it never really dawned on me until I was at the end of my tether. Jesus is my Saviour. He is my Lord and my God. As I sat in my armchair, I began to cling to Him for dear life. And it was only afterward that I recognized that He was the One who held me safely in His grip first. By His Spirit, working with His Word, the Father had revealed the Son to me. The Spirit enabled me to see the Father in the Son, Jesus Christ. Jesus is the way to God. He is the Truth. He is objective truth – truth outside of me, outside of all men. And He is the Life – everlasting life. Jesus is Paradise. He is Noah's Ark. He is Solomon's Temple. He is Salvation.

> Though the fig tree may not blossom, nor fruit be on the vines; though the labor of the olive may fail, and the fields yield no food; though the flock may be cut off from the fold, and there be no herd in the stalls – yet I will rejoice in the LORD, I will joy in the God of my salvation. The LORD God [i.e., Jehovah Adonai] is my strength; He will make my feet like deer's feet, and He will make me walk on my high hills. (Hab. 3:17-19)

> 1) There came a Shepherd long ago,
>   Searching for His sheep.
>   He will not rest till all His flock
>   Is safely in His keep.
>   With open arms He calls to them.
>   His voice is soft yet clear.
>   And they come home to Him again.
>   The Shepherd loves them dear.
>   Good Shepherd I will heed Your call,
>   For this I must confess:
>   I cannot find my own way out
>   Of this darkened wilderness.
>   – Author

Further Solomonic Insight

*W*INNIPEG winters are bitter to the bone, icing up the very marrow to brittleness. The locals affectionately refer to their prairie city – their "bump in the snow" – as "Winterpeg"!

Spring was very much appreciated by me when its warm hand would pull back the shroud of snow and bring the land back to life. The warm breath of God breathes life into the nostrils of the land, and Solomon's beautiful Shulamite says, "My beloved spoke, and said to me: 'Rise up, my love, my fair one, and come away. For lo, the winter is past, the rain is over and gone. The flowers appear on the earth; the time of singing has come, and the voice of the turtle dove is heard in our land'" (Song of Sol. 2:10–12).

My beloved Dorothy and I would sit at the front of our house on Molson Street to catch the sun's benign rays as it warmed the morning. Our children would play on the front path under our watchful and doting eyes. Their laughter tinkled in our hearts like wind chimes swaying in a gentle breeze.

I planted some nasturtiums and sweet peas just under our living room window, next to the front step where we would sit together. To keep the house cool, I had hung a roll-down blind over the window that blessed the living room with a bit of shade. The blind had a leafy bamboo pattern on it.

One morning I was in the living room and could see some little shadows dancing on the blind. I thought that, though unusual to see them in the sun, they were the flutterings of large moths. Butterflies? Too solid-seeming for them. The shadows seemed to dance, then defy gravity with one-spot hovering. I peered out the window to see beautifully coloured hummingbirds sampling the cool nectar of the flowering sweet peas and nasturtiums. Oh how can a desolate barren winter-land become such a living, breathing organism in spring, blooming into summer fullness? A time for singing indeed! Balance! Life! Harmony!

God is good!

Welding Pen (Sheep Pen)

*I*N the course of time, I began telling my Masonic friends all about Jesus, "the stone the builders rejected." I began to tell my workmates at the railway about Jesus. They could see a change in me. Immediately my "taking the Lord's name in vain" ceased, and then soon all profanity from my speech.

I had known for some time that some Christians gathered at lunchtime in one of the welding pens (shielded enclosures). We referred to them derogatorily as "sheep in their sheep pen." I saw one of them on the shop floor. He just about dropped dead when I asked if I could join them for lunch in their "sheep pen." The others welcomed me like a long-lost son. Usually there were only about four or five of them. One of them would read a few verses of Scripture and we would have a bit of discussion and pray.

One time, one of the men (a fellow Scot) whose job it was to hand out the tools to the boilermakers and pipefitters, noticing I was missing from the usual crowd, asked where I kept on disappearing to at lunchtime. He was told that I was congregating with the "Holy Willies." He wasn't a Christian, but he asked if he could join us! I invited him home for a meal the coming Friday evening. Next day, I took him to a Christian men's breakfast.

I spent the rest of our time after breakfast telling him everything I knew about Jesus and salvation. I took him with me to church on the following Sunday morning. He picked up some Christian tracts and brochures. On Monday, as I was walking past his tool crib (where he had been contemplating what had been taught to him over the weekend), he began excitedly to declare "I know who Jesus is! I know who Jesus is!" I looked at him straight in the eye and said, "Don't forget who you were before this moment!" He went on to become a solid Christian.

> Make me a captive, Lord,
> And then I shall be free;
> Force me to render up my sword,

And I shall a conqueror be.
I sink in life's alarms
When by myself I stand;
Imprison me within Thine arms,
And strong shall be my hand.

– George Matheson (1842–1906)
Hymn 464, RCH

My Mum's Passing

I WAS called into the office of the department of the Canadian National Railway where I worked. I was told to phone home, it was urgent. Dorothy told me that my mum had just died. My legs buckled beneath me. My foreman joked about me making an excuse so I could go home immediately. I hadn't told him that my mother had just died, only that I had to go home straightaway.

Outside the railway plant, the sky was blue but the air was bitterly cold – minus thirty-odd degrees or so Celsius. I unplugged the electric cable Winnipegers use to keep the car oil warm. My car started without any trouble. It happened as I turned onto Regent's Avenue: the car's heater sprang a leak under the dashboard and its spray-mist was freezing as it hit the inside of the windshield. I was dazed enough without this to contend with! I used the scraper normally reserved for scraping ice off the *outside* of the windshield. I should have stopped my car but I just wanted to get home to be with my wife. So, with one hand holding the steering wheel, I kept scraping the inside of the iced-up windshield to keep clear a peephole as I drove home to Molson Street in North Kildonan.

It was decided that I should fly back to Scotland to be with my family and attend my mum's funeral. As a new Christian, I handled the test well. I trusted in the Lord to get me through the ordeal of losing a loved one. He upheld me in His everlasting arms.

My mother died of cancer in 1989, twelve years after I had left Scotland for Canada. While back for the funeral, I caught up with some old friends and acquaintances. I had a look at the plumbing yard on North Street, Alexandria, where I used to work. I even went to McKenzie's pub at the top of North Street for a pint. Friday used to be our payday. And it used to be a good opportunity to catch up with the other tradesmen and talk over a pint or two about the past week's activities and those planned for the weekend.

I looked around at the faces in the pub as I leaned nostalgically on the bar. I recognized a man on the other side of the bar. Our eyes locked. He said he hadn't seen me around for a while and asked if I had moved to Dumbarton (a town about four miles away). He just about dropped his pint on the floor when I told him I had been in Canada twelve years. Time flies! The man told me that he was preparing to move to Australia. So was I.

Postcards from Australia

THE Winnipeg winters were getting harder and harder for me to thole.* I loved the hot Manitoba summers, but they would end all too soon. And then after the brief "Indian Summer" in September, a sense of foreboding would seep into the very marrow of my bones, for then it was time to start to batten down the hatches for the long, hard battle with winter.

Sometimes it would begin to snow early, one time even on my eldest daughter Jennifer's birthday on October 8. Usually the month of October was when the temperature would begin to plummet. By

---

* Thole: Scottish; *suffer* or *endure*.

Halloween or the October 31st Reformation Day, the snows had well and truly arrived and would invariably outstay their welcome until the end of April of the next year. The same snow could lie on the ground from October to April without melting once! The Manitoba farmers delighted in the snow, for they depended on the volume of melted snow in spring to moisturize their fields for crop planting.

Shovelling paths and driveways became the exercise regime for all. That pathway to our mailbox had to be kept clear lest the mailman refuse to deliver! Dorothy showed me some photographs she received in a letter from her brother who had moved to Brisbane, Australia. I asked about the dark-coloured man in the picture. "That's my brother Alan!" she said. Alan, sporting a glorious suntan, was surrounded by palm trees, golden sands, and a turquoise ocean.

We applied to migrate to Australia and were accepted after being made to jump over many hurdles and pass through many hoops. Alan was going to put us up in his Brisbane flat. I had begun to pray that the Lord would gather Dorothy's family together. Her mum and her sister still lived in Scotland. We were in Australia for a year when her sister Elizabeth and her husband Robert arrived to stay. Then came Margaret, her mum!

Part Three

Ministry

Australia

*A*s were the first President of the United States of America, George Washington, and the first Prime Minister of Canada, Sir John A. MacDonald, so was the first Prime Minister of Australia, Sir Edmund Barton (1849–1920) – all Freemasons. Barton was Prime Minister of Australia from 1901 to '03. And like the United States of America and Canada, Australia, too, has a rich Christian heritage. The laws at the founding of these three nations were based upon the Ten Commandments.

Australia came by its name on account of explorers. I admire explorers. I love their risk-taking sense of adventure! One such was the Portuguese-born explorer for the King of Spain, Pedro Fernandez de Quiros (1563–1615). Apparently, it was through him that Australia got her name in a mixed-up sort of a way.

Ptolemy in 150 B.C. showed on his maps a southern land he called *Terra Australis Incognita*, Latin for "the unknown land of the South." Quiros discovered Vanuatu, and, thinking that the island on which he landed was part of that great southern continent, named it *Austrialia del Espiritu Santo*, Latin for "Southland of the Holy Spirit," saying, "Let the heavens, the earth, the waters with all their creatures and all those here present witness that I, Captain Pedro Fernandez de Quiros, in these hitherto unknown parts, in the name of Jesus Christ, Son of the Eternal Father, and of the Virgin Mary, God and true man, hoist this emblem of the Holy Cross on which His person was crucified and whereon He gave His life for the ransom and remedy of all the human race, being present as witnesses all the land and sea-going officers; on this Day of Pentecost, 14 May 1606."

Matthew Flinders (1774–1814) was the first man to circumnavigate Australia. Regardless whether Australia derives her name from Austria after Philip III of Spain (a prince of the House of Austria) via Pedro Fernandez de Quiros, or from Ptolemy and the ancient cartographer's *Terra Australis Incognita*, it was Flinders who suggested the simple name "Australia," which was adopted in 1824. Flinders, wrote in his *Voyage to Terra Australis* (1814), "Had I permitted myself any innovation upon the original term *Terra Australis*, it would have been to convert it into *Australia*." Several places have been named after him such as Flinders Island off the northern tip of Tasmania. Flinders was yet another Freemason!*

Robert O'Hara Burke (1820–61) and William John Wills (1834–61) or, simply, "Burke and Wills," were two famous explorers of inland Australia who perished on one of their expeditions (www.burke andwills.org/). A fellow Scot (and namesake of mine) was sent to find out what had happened to them. John McKinlay (1819–72) was born in Sandybank on the Holy Loch, Argyllshire, Scotland. He and his brother Alexander migrated to New South Wales in 1836. John learned the art of bushcraft from the Aboriginal people. It is said that he was "thoroughly self-reliant, an accurate shot, and equal to almost any situation except public speaking." It would seem that McKinlay was well suited for the task of finding the two missing explorers – but not for *explaining* to others what he found on his travels!

Whether exploring the inland continent of Australia, outer space, molecular structures, oceanic depths – are we not simply seeking knowledge of God? Are not microscopes and telescopes simply instruments pointed toward the God of Creation?

1) The earth belongs unto the Lord,
   and all that it contains;
   The world that is inhabited,
   and all that there remains.

2) For the foundations thereof
   He on the seas did lay,
   And He hath it established
   upon the floods to stay.

— Psalm 24, RCH

* www.swcs.com.au/aust2.htm

Pacific Roar

*A*USTRALIA had been well explored and well-settled by the time I arrived in Brisbane with my wife Dorothy and our three daughters in October 1990. The jacaranda trees were in full bloom, offering cool shade from the hot sun. And, as if to welcome us to Australia, their periwinkle-coloured petals sprinkled the paths we walked upon. Jennifer was eight, and the twins, Nina, and Fionna, were just four. Dorothy's brother, Alan, put us up in his flat at Toowong. He took us on many sightseeing trips and helped us to get acquainted with our new home.

I'll never forget our first trip to the beach at the Gold Coast. We couldn't see the beach from where we had parked the car, having to walk over a giant sand dune of sorts. As we crested the dune, I experienced again what I had sensed on the shore of that Great Lake in Canada some thirteen years before – only multiplied a hundredfold! On first sight, the sheer vastness of the Pacific Ocean crushed me to insignificance. The roar of the constant onslaught of majestic breakers was deafening as they baptized the golden shore. I trembled before God and thanked Him. "Let the sea roar, and all its fullness, the world and those who dwell in it; let the rivers clap their hands; let the hills be joyful together before the LORD, for He is coming to judge the earth. With righteousness He shall judge the world, and the peoples with equity" (Psalm 98:7–9). I wrote the following rhyme:

> If anyone should ask you,
> What became of me,
> Tell them I'm Down Under
> The Jacaranda tree!

"Best Laid Schemes
o' Mice and Men"

THE plan was for me to find employment as a plumber in Australia. This wasn't as easy as first anticipated. One of the reasons we had been accepted – and the main reason we had decided to become migrants to Australia – was on account of the country's need for plumbers. The deal when I arrived was that I had to work for three months with a plumbing company before I would be given an Australian plumbing licence. I had plumbing certificates and licences from both Canada and Scotland (City and Guilds).

I had a great deal of trouble getting an Australian plumbing licence due to the fact that every job I applied for required that the applicant already have a plumbing licence! Therefore, I couldn't get a job because I didn't have a licence, and couldn't get a licence because I didn't have a job! I decided to do something useful with my spare time.

I had been attending the Christian Reformed Church where we lived in Toowong. The church didn't have its own minister at that time and would invite preachers to come along to take the worship service on Sunday. I was delighted one Sunday morning to meet the visiting preacher who was about to lead us in the worship of God. Upon hearing my accent, he immediately engaged me in a conversation about all things Scottish. He was an encyclopaedia of knowledge.

He mounted the pulpit and began to show me and the rest of the congregation the very thing we needed, i.e., the very One I had been looking for when I was in the Masonic lodge. He presented Christ to us, but in such a way that I could sense and see my wretched unworthiness. I could see Christ's holiness as the second Person in the Trinity – but how could I draw near to a holy God? Then the preacher showed us the grace of God in Jesus Christ, and I began to clearly see God's grace in Christ's loveliness as He drew me to Himself like a long-lost brother. What a humble Saviour!

For, on account of the blood Jesus Christ shed on the cross, God is pleased to welcome a sinner like me into His holy presence!

After illustrating the holiness of God and His graciousness to sinners, the preacher went on to tell us that there is a future day coming when all the redeemed will be like Jesus. By this the preacher meant that, just as Christ Jesus had been resurrected bodily, so we shall be physically resurrected from our graves. Then we shall be like Jesus – a resurrected and regenerated 33-year-old! On that day, we shall be without sin, and without the effects of the curse that presently weigh us down body and soul. Also, we shall indeed be included in God's new creation, i.e., the re-created earth where the resurrected Jesus will dwell in the midst of us forever!

Well, this was like nothing I had ever heard preached before! Yet, at home afterwards, when I searched the Scriptures to see if these things were so, I could see that the preacher spoke God's Gospel truth! It was then that I could see for the first time that becoming a Christian is about much, much more than simply going to some nebulous place called Heaven when you die. Rather, I was beginning to learn that the life Christ has purchased for us is about glorifying God by delighting in Him and cultivating His creation now! Life is about serving Him every moment and not just worshipping Him for an hour on Sundays.

I set my heart to pray that God would raise up preachers like the preacher I had just heard: preachers who, by showing the holiness of God, would enable their congregations to see the blackness of their own sinful hearts for breaking God's Law, yet, at the same time, point them to God's grace for the forgiveness of sin found only in Jesus Christ, all this while also exhorting us to live every aspect of our lives to the glory of God. Big task, but God is Almighty, and God can change hearts.

He changed mine!

The Day the Universe Changed

*E*VERY Saturday I was sure to purchase the *Brisbane Courier Mail* in order to review its classified ads. Religiously I would scan the job section for plumbing jobs. One time, in the course of inquiring over the phone about the requirements for one of the jobs advertised, I asked the person on the other end of the line what he meant by a "ute." The advert said, "Must have own ute." "What's a ute?" I asked. The voice on the other end replied with a question, "Mate, how long have you been in Australia?" "I've just arrived," I told him. "I can tell!" and with that he was gone! It turns out that a "ute" is abbreviated speak for a utility truck!

Still, I persisted in studying newspaper job ads. One time I had laid the opened paper on the carpet as I sat on the couch leaning over it. I noticed that the edge of the large newspaper lined up with a shadow the bright sun was casting on the living room floor. As I studied the jobs section, (like a good Mason!) I would move the edge of the paper to keep it square – in line– with the shadow as it slowly moved across the floor. Suddenly it dawned on me. The shadow was moving the wrong way! I went out onto the porch to ascertain the cause of my alarm.

The people walking past outside didn't seem to mind at all that the sun was doing something very strange that day. As it turns out, in the southern hemisphere the sun rises in the east, goes by way of the north– not by way of the south as I had grown used to while living in the northern hemisphere– and sets in the west. Trying to come to terms with this was a lesson on its own. Clearly I was in Australia, the land "down under"!

The sun casting shadows on my sense of reality served to help me get lost while driving the old worn-out station wagon I eventually purchased. Ordinarily I would use the sun and the time of day to get a rough idea as to direction. But with the shadows moving the "wrong" direction, the equation became too hard for me to calculate. Often I wouldn't even know which direction I was travelling though I was following the road shown on the map!

Which Church?

ONE of the major problems I was confronted with after my armchair conversion was which church I should attend. I knew instinctively and, more so from reading the Bible, that I should be attending Sunday worship somewhere. But finding a God-honouring church is a minefield if there ever was one! I had, as I searched for God, found myself one Easter morning sitting in the anti-Trinitarian Kingdom Hall of the Jehovah's Witnesses. The people there were really nice and friendly, but that isn't what it's all about. I needed spiritual food! I just wanted to attend a place where I could worship God and be taught clearly what God is saying in His Word. No spin!

I wandered from church to church. Some "preachers" seemed more interested in talking about the voices they had heard or the visions they had seen, than telling their congregations what God has already revealed in His Word. All I wanted was to hear the Scriptures expounded!

Back in Winnipeg, I had eventually settled into a downtown church where the Word was faithfully expounded each Lord's Day. They styled themselves as a non-denominational church, therefore it was nigh impossible to find a church like them in Australia. I had been taking my eldest daughter Jennifer (who was 6 at the time) to the local public swimming pool on Sunday mornings. I began to take her, with Nina and Fionna, her 2-year-old twin sisters, to that non-denominational church instead.

Upon arrival in Australia, I arose early on our first Sunday morning, read some verses of Scripture, and prayed that God would help me find a church. I planned to walk around the area until I found one. As I crested a hill, I heard what distantly sounded a little like hymns being sung. I went to investigate. I didn't have time to read the noticeboard before I was whisked inside and was seated next to a Scotsman who had been in Australia for many years.

The next thing I knew the worship service had begun. A man was walking back and forth up in the front speaking in what I, at the time, thought must be Old Testament Hebrew or New Testament

Greek. It was weird for me. I couldn't understand what the preacher was saying. Though I had Pentecostal friends, I had never heard anyone speak in "tongues." Next the man was laying hands on the people who had made their way to him for healing.

I just wanted to bolt the course, but when the service finished, the man next to me asked how I had "enjoyed" the service. I told him that I thought that it was going okay right up to the point where the preacher started talking what had sounded, to my untrained ear, like gibberish! I told him that I couldn't understand a word of it. Well, the man didn't take too kindly to my comment and said that he knew of someone who had held a view similar to mine to whom some terrible fate befell! He withdrew himself from me and I made with all haste for the exit.

I was almost out of the building when the preacher intercepted me. He too asked what I thought of the service. Still in shock by what the other man had said to me, I attempted to tell him what I had already told the other man. Thankfully, I will say that the preacher was far more gracious and patient with me, the fairly new Christian, and asked if we could get together and talk about it. I left him my phone number.

I was really shaken by the threat the first man had made to me. As I stepped out of the door of the church building and onto the street a blinding flash of lightning and an accompanying ear-piercing thunderclap met me as my foot met with the sidewalk! I really thought that God for some reason was going to "do-me-in"! I was sure I was going to be run over by a car or struck by lightning or meet with some terrible fate on the way home.

When I arrived home safely, I read my Bible the whole day, in preparation for the meeting with the preacher. That phone call never came. However, it seemed to me that one of two things had taken place. Either the devil was trying to scare me away from church or God was using this experience to help instil in me the need to test all things against Scripture (Isa. 8:20; Acts 17:11). Believing in the sovereignty of God I opted for the latter!

I read in 1 Corinthians 14:13 that the preacher, to have been

Biblical, should have had someone interpret what he was saying. I also learned therefore that not all churches are fully Biblical in practice. However, (as explained later in this book), I did eventually find a church that suited me.

The following Sunday, as my search continued, I attended a Chinese Christian church. I decided not to go back there either, because I thought that it was on account of the fact that I didn't speak Cantonese that they had to translate their tongues-speaking. How could I do that to them? It would double the length of their worship service! Only later did I discover that they conducted every worship service in Cantonese with English translation!

It seems to me that the problem at the first church could have been solved if only that preacher had someone to give interpretation of his "other tongue."

1) The Church's one foundation
   Is Jesus Christ her Lord:
   She is His new creation
   By water and the Word;
   From heaven He came and sought her
   To be His holy bride;
   With His own blood He bought her,
   And for her life He died.

3) Though with a scornful wonder
   men see her sore oppressed,
   by schisms rent asunder,
   by heresies distressed.
   Yet saints their watch are keeping,
   Their cry goes up, "How long?"
   And soon the night of weeping
   Shall be the morn of song.
   — Samuel John Stone (1839–1900)
   Hymn 205, RCH

By Road and By Sea

ONE time my eldest daughter Jennifer and I took the coast road and drove from Brisbane, Queensland, all the way to Hobart, Tasmania. Jennifer's bright and bubbly personality and her intelligent conversation made for a great trip as we shared the driving. We had Wee Jamie, our Sydney Silky terrier, with us. Jamie was really just an overgrown Yorkie! Like most other dogs, he loved travelling in cars. And I suppose like most other dogs, he didn't like air-conditioning, preferring fast-moving cars with rolled-down windows so that he could thrust his hairy face into the onrushing wind. What is it with dogs and car windows? As we drove along, seeing Wee Jamie's face in my side mirror with all his whiskers blowing in the wind reminded me of Chewbacca in the *Star Wars* movies.

We travelled south through Sydney and then curved west round the coast to Melbourne where we wanted to catch the ferry across Bass Strait to the Apple Isle. We were four days on the road and we both appreciated the Australian countryside as it passed by.

Sadly, one of the things you notice when travelling in different countries is the different variety of road-kill. In Scotland, it was usually rabbits, squirrels, hedgehogs, assorted birds, and maybe the occasional deer that littered the roadside. In Canada, it was mostly chipmunks, squirrels, raccoons, assorted birds, and deer. Mind you, I don't recall ever seeing a dead moose at the side of a road in Canada – and if a car and moose did collide, most cars would come off second best! Australia's country roads are littered mainly with wallabies, wombats, koalas, and possums by the score – not forgetting the variety of birds of bright and colourful plumage. It's such a shame!

To the traveller, trees in Scotland and Canada tend to be similar in appearance: a proliferation of conifers interspersed with a variety of the usual leaf-shedding deciduous. In Australia, the strong and distinct smell of gum trees filled the car whenever we rolled down a window for the benefit of Wee Jamie.

On the coast road, the sea views would snatch your breath away.

On the land side, it was a veritable Garden of Eden with a great many clearings opening up into bright and beautiful vistas of very arable farmland. I became "theologically challenged" as we drove through a small town in southern New South Wales. The town was called Eden, and it had a sawmill. I had pictures going through my mind of Adam in the Garden of Eden sawing the tall trees of Eden into planks. As I thought about it along our journey, I concluded that though Adam the Gardener became "Farmer Adam" after he ate the forbidden fruit, Adam the "Woodwright" working in an "Eden's Sawmill" wouldn't be too far off the truth – Cultural Mandate taken into consideration and all of that!

The eight-hour overnight trip on the *Spirit of Tasmania* across Bass Strait from Melbourne, Victoria, to Devonport, Tasmania, was brilliant! There's something about being on a ship that is special to me – perhaps sailing is in my blood. I have a photograph that belonged to my dad of his Canadian-built ship *The Fort Spokane* as it was going under the Sydney Harbour Bridge. The "Coat Hanger," as the bridge is called by locals because of its steel-arch design, is clearly seen in the photo. Some entrepreneurial photographer snapped it and was selling copies of it to the ship's sailors as they spilled ashore.

The photograph used to hang on the wall of the living room of the McKinlay family home; then on the wall of the Frank Downie Old Folk's Home in Dalmuir, Scotland, where my dad lived for a short time just before he died. It had the following note attached to it, written in my father's own script: THE FORT SPOKANE, *a Canadian built Liberty Ship. I signed on in Port Pirie, Australia and sailed to Tasmania and round the Cape of Good Hope, South Africa to Liverpool.*

As we sailed across Bass Strait, I was both enchanted and enamoured, alternating between studying the starry night sky above, and watching the swirls and eddies being ploughed up by the ship's bow in the inky-black water below. Above, I could see the well-known Plough (Big Dipper), and Pleiades (the Seven Sisters). I could also see the constellation that is not visible from the northern hemisphere – that which is emblazoned on the Australian national flag, the great reminder of her Christian heritage – the Southern Cross.

As I took three deep breaths of fresh air into my lungs, I thought of my dad in his navy days. His trip to the island of Tasmania was made in the late 1940s. I thought of Noah and his great ship. I also thought of a Masonic lodge I once belonged to. I had been initiated into Freemasonry in a lodge called Seven Stars. I had come a long way; and with my eldest daughter with me, it was great to be alive!

Being Reformed

THE Christian Reformed Church of Australia came into being in the early 1950s. It was formed primarily by Dutch migrants and their offspring who did not wish to become part of the Presbyterian Church of Australia (1901) on account of that denomination's tolerance of Freemasonry, which, at that time, was prevalent in her midst!

I didn't know I was a theologically "reformed" Christian until I sat in the Reformed Church in Toowong! The first time I was there, I was thumbing through one of their hymnbooks before the Sunday morning service of worship began. It had a copy of the Heidelberg Catechism in it. As I read the Catechism, tears began to fill my eyes! I thought to myself, "If these people believe what is written in their Catechism, then I have arrived home!" The Catechism spelled out, in warm pastoral language, what Christians believe. There was no guessing. It was written down for all to read. I asked if I could take it home to study it. The favour was granted.

I had been used to churches that viewed the children of believers as little "goats," and not the Lord's little lambs. So I took the elders of the Toowong Reformed Church to task for their view of baptizing the infants of believers. The men were very patient with me. They didn't pronounce a curse on me like the man in the first church I had attended in Australia! Again, for me it was to "the law and to the testimony! If they do not speak according to this word it is because there is no light in them" (Isa. 8:20).

I searched the Scriptures and found that New Testament baptism means the same as Old Testament circumcision, that both are different administrations of the same Covenant of Grace. Old Testament males (including their infants), as lawful members of the covenant community, received the sign and seal as it was administered then, i.e., circumcision. New Testament male and female members of the same covenant community receive the sign and seal as instituted by Christ, i.e., water baptism.

Colossians 2 verses 11 and 12 clinched it for me, for there Paul demonstrates that New Testament baptism has superseded Old Testament circumcision. The Heidelberg Catechism states what the Bible teaches thus:

Q & A 72

Q. Is, then, the outward washing with water itself the washing away of sin?

A. No, for only the blood of Jesus Christ and the Holy Spirit cleanse us from all sins.

Q & A 73

Q. Why, then, does the Holy Spirit call baptism the washing of regeneration and the washing away of sins?

A. God speaks thus not without great cause: to wit, not only to teach us thereby that as the filthiness of the body is taken away by water, so our sins are removed by the blood and Spirit of Jesus Christ; but especially to assure us by this divine pledge and sign that we are spiritually cleansed from our sins as really as we are outwardly washed with water.

Q & A 74

Q. Are infants also to be baptized?

A. Yes; for since they, as well as adults, are included in the covenant and Church of God, and since both redemption from sin and the Holy Spirit, the Author of faith, are through the blood of Christ promised to them no less than to adults, they must also by baptism, as a sign of the covenant, be ingrafted into the Christian Church, and distinguished from the children of unbelievers, as was done in the old covenant or testament by circumcision, instead of which baptism was instituted in the new covenant.

I approached the elders of the Toowong Christian Reformed Church and asked if my three daughters and I could be baptized since none of us had ever been baptized. After meeting with a learned elder for instruction for six months or more, I and my three daughters were duly baptized by a minister of the Christian Reformed Church on Sunday, June 30, 1991. I asked the elder who was teaching me if everyone who wanted to become a member of the Reformed Church had to go through such an in-depth theological course before being baptized. I was told that there was always instruction, but it wasn't usually the case that it was so in-depth. I was told that they were trying to feed my insatiable appetite for Bible understanding. I wanted to know God and the things of God. These elders were helping me!

> 1) Guide me, O Thou great Jehovah,
>   Pilgrim through this barren land;
>   I am weak, but Thou art mighty;
>   Hold me with Thy powerful hand:
>   Bread of heaven,
>   Feed me till my want is o'er.
>
>   – William Williams (1717–1791)
>   Translated by Peter Williams
>   Hymn 564, RCH

Dorothy's Conversion

I CONTINUED attending the Toowong Christian Reformed Church even after we had moved to a rented place in Browns Plains, a 35-minute drive away.

Hearing of my skills as a handyman, the property owner offered me the task of building a wooden fence around the fairly large backyard of our Browns Plains home. It was while I was sawing a piece of timber that I came under a very strong conviction. I couldn't stop thinking about the type of preaching I had heard by the visiting preacher at Toowong. I had been praying fervently that God would raise up other men to preach in the way that I had heard that man preach. I began thinking to myself as I sawed through that piece of wood, "Me? I could never stand in front of people and speak! I have a very different accent. Australians would never understand me!" My real coup de grace (or so I thought!) that would disqualify me from the terrifying prospect of preaching in front of people was that my wife was not a Christian. Therefore, how could I possibly lead a congregation of Christians when my own wife had no love for God and Christ?

Our marriage was becoming strained on account of my zeal for the things of God and Dorothy's lack thereof. Dorothy had a plan. She had spotted a signpost pointing to a Presbyterian church up the road from where we now lived. She remembered attending a Presbyterian church in Scotland (i.e., Church of Scotland). She remembered the congregation to be what she called "normal Christians," i.e., not like the type of Christian I was. Those normal Christians at the church she had attended as a child in Scotland would let their children "play" séances – even while at church! According to her, no one there believed the Bible stuff I was coming out with! She thought that if only she could get me to attend a "normal" church, perhaps I would give up my "foolish beliefs"!

One evening I went to check out the Presbyterian church along the road from where we lived. I was more than happy with what I heard preached. The preacher simply took the Bible, read a passage from it, and then began to explain and apply that passage of Scripture to us. No gobbledygook, no theatrics, just the Bible, hymn singing, and prayer. This is what I had grown used to in the Toowong Christian Reformed Church.

Since the church at Toowong didn't have an evening service, I became a regular attendee of the Browns Plains Presbyterian Church's evening service. With a great deal of sad reluctance, but with their eventual blessing, the elders of Toowong Christian Reformed Church allowed me to transfer my church membership to the Browns Plains Presbyterian Church, which is part of a greater body called the Presbyterian Church of Queensland, which, again, is a member of the Presbyterian Church of Australia.

Dorothy began to attend the morning worship service with the children and me. At the time, she had been reading a novel by Frank E. Peretti called *This Present Darkness* that I had purchased in Canada just a few months before we departed for Australia. This very entertaining piece of fiction deals with spiritual warfare from a Pentecostal perspective. Righteous angels fight against demonic forces that are attempting to take over a small town in America. The book's premise served to awaken Dorothy to the idea of good and evil in the world and how people are influenced in their beliefs and actions. As a result of Peretti's tale, Dorothy became interested in the things of God as revealed in the Bible.

One Sunday morning at church, I happened to notice that Dorothy was listening very attentively to the sermon as the preacher showed the congregation the connection between what Adam had done in the Garden of Eden and what Christ had done on the cross. With this "Gospel thread" running through it from the beginning to the end, the whole Bible began to make a lot more sense to her. I could see that "the lights" were being turned on for my wife. No more glazed-over-look that Christians see in non-Christians as sometimes happens when we talk to them about the things of God! Now our marriage was back on track, rock solid! (Thank You, Lord, for my wife's conversion!)

Sawing Logs

IT'S funny how doing certain actions can trigger memories. As I sawed through planks of wood to build the backyard fence, I could hear my dad's voice as plain as day: "Let the saw do the work, son." It seems that all that is needed to cut a piece of timber is a sharp saw. My dad learned an important lesson about saws the hard way. (No, he didn't cut off any fingers!)

One time when he was a lad, he was having trouble cutting through a piece of wood. He closely examined the saw blade to see what the problem was. *Aha! The teeth are all crooked*, he thought to himself. So he took his hammer, laid the saw against some concrete and proceeded to straighten out those crooked teeth. However, this only made the blunt saw even more blunt. Apparently the teeth are supposed to be crooked – one this way, and the next that way. It's part of the design for how the device works. I thought this was hilarious! So every time I pick up a saw, I chuckle! Mind you, letting the saw do the work was analogous of my father's philosophy of life, which, put aphoristically, is this: *Man must not serve the machine; the machine must serve man.*

I got to thinking about how I perceived the political philosophy my dad once held. Like giant mechanical earthworms in some Japanese horror movie, ever expanding cities ate up the surrounding arable farmland at the advent of the industrial revolution. Here man began to serve the machine as he was fed into its productive output. Marx saw this in terms of dialectical materialism where thesis and antithesis gobble up each other and produce a synthetic waste product (a sludge of drudge!) that, in turn, becomes the thesis.

If the thesis is viewed as man, and if the antithesis of man is the machine, then a synthesis of man and machine is the new thesis. But isn't this simply the snake – or the mechanical earthworm – disappearing on account of swallowing its own tail? The dialectic is its own destruction. Therefore, isn't the synthesis of man and machine the eventual annihilation of both? In Marxism, the State becomes a "leviathan" (as in the book *Leviathan* by Thomas Hobbes, 1651) swallowing up every last vestige of human freedom.

Marx's problem was that he was a materialist. Thus, because Marx had excluded God, his presupposition about the history of man was based on a faulty premise. Faulty foundations mean walls will topple (consider Berlin). Marx had forgotten that the history of man includes the fall of man. But though man rebelled against God and fell, we see exemplified with Solomon building the Temple, solid foundational work. Solomon's work rested on strong foundations because it was a work done to the glory of God. There were hundreds of thousands of people involved in the Temple's construction – from lumberjacks sawing down trees in Lebanon, to gold-leaf workers on site in Jerusalem.

There was peace. There was no rage against "the system." There was no revolution. There was only peace throughout the land. It was a time of harmony – a time when man honoured his Maker – a time when man "let the saw to do the work."

Called to the Ministry

I SOUGHT work in Australia. But, seeing as I couldn't get a plumbing job – (because I didn't have an Australian plumbing licence and couldn't get an Australian plumbing licence because I didn't have a job) – and because I was interested in theology, I sought to enrol as a private student at the Queensland Theological College in Brisbane. This Presbyterian college was usually referred to as "the Hall." With some negotiation, I qualified to receive a small bursary [scholarship] and began to study New Testament Greek, Church History, and other Biblical subjects.

The events that led up to this were varied. Dorothy had landed a temporary job for six months with the Australian Government.

I stayed at home watching Nina and Fionna who were too young to attend school with Jennifer. So the girls "helped" me with my carpentry work of building the wooden backyard fence.

One Monday morning, the preacher for the Browns Plains Presbyterian Church came to my house and asked if I would like to preach at the Sunday evening service. I asked what I had to do! He basically said that all I needed to do was make a few scribbles on a piece of paper as notes and explain and apply some portion of Scripture to the congregation!

At the Sunday evening worship service I attempted to do just that. It was the most nerve-wracking thing I've ever had to go through! I stood white as a sheet before all these people with my reading glasses sliding off my face because I was sweating profusely! I basically read the scribbles on my wee piece of paper and passed a few comments and my sermon was done in all of five minutes! Apparently, the Session of Elders (governing council) at church saw something in me that I couldn't see, and then one thing led to another.

I had got hold of the phone number of the preacher I had previously encountered at the Toowong Christian Reformed Church. I dialled his number and he answered. It had been some weeks, maybe months, but I was pleased that he remembered speaking to me when he had visited church to preach that Sunday morning. In the course of our conversation I asked if he knew how to tell when a man was being called to the ministry. There was a silent pause on the other end of the line. He then asked me if I knew to whom I was speaking. I had to admit that I didn't have a clue, apart from knowing that he was a preacher! He told me that he was the Reverend Professor Doctor Francis Nigel Lee, and that his job at the Presbyterian Church of Queensland's Theological College (i.e., the Hall) was to help teach men how to become good ministers!

I soon had no excuses as to why I could not become a minister of Christ's Gospel. I had the support of the Session of Elders and congregation of my local church at Browns Plains. I had passed the examination of the Presbytery to which the local church belonged, and had also been accepted by the college faculty. My personal plan was to take stock at the end of each year. If I passed all the college exams and assignments, I would continue into the next year.

The study regime was most grueling, and the learning curve was not "curved" but rather a sheer cliff-face for me. Before I went to college, I had read the many Christian books my brother Fearghas had sent me from Scotland. At the time I read them, I had no idea that their authors were predominantly Reformed and Presbyterian, i.e., Calvinist authors such as Cornelius Van Til, R. B. Kuiper, E. J. Young, Francis Schaeffer, and Herman Bavinck. No wonder I fit in so well in Reformed and Presbyterian circles!

At the end of my final year, on graduation night at the big brick Presbyterian church in downtown Brisbane, I was taken by surprise when I heard my name being called out to come up to the front to receive that year's award for homiletics (i.e., preaching). God had answered my prayers to raise up preachers by raising up me! That clinched and confirmed my call to the ministry, not to mention an incident at the door afterwards. As we were shaking the multitude's collection of hands at the door after the service, a woman asked me if I remembered preaching as a guest student preacher at her church one Sunday evening. She said that the God of grace had really opened her eyes that night and she had been saved! She asked if I could remember the text I preached on that night. It was John 14:6, "I am the way, the truth, and the life. No one comes to the Father except through Me."

Christ Honoured at Australia's Centre

J ADMIRE John Flynn (1880–1951) who in earlier times was also called to be a minister in the Presbyterian Church of Australia. He was the founder of the Australian Inland Mission (AIM) now called the Presbyterian Inland Mission (PIM). Flynn is best known as the founder of the Flying Doctor Service of Australia serving especially the remote Red Centre (or Outback) regions of Australia. I was surprised to discover that Flynn also had a Canadian connection, for, in 1940 and '41, the degrees of Doctor of Divinity were conferred on him by the University of Toronto and the Presbyterian College at McGill University, Montreal. Flynn's remains are buried at the foot of Mount Gillen in Alice Springs.

Rev. Terry Saddler, a PIM "padre," was telling me about something he had discovered in the vicinity of Lambert's Centre of Australia, just south of Alice Springs. Lambert's Centre of Australia is the point at which if a pin with a string were stuck into the middle of an aerial map of Australia, Lambert's Centre would be the place at which Australia would find its balance. It was very near this point that Terry came across a grave marked by a simple marble headstone. The headstone, according to Terry, had broken into three pieces but had then been set upright and wired together using two star-pickets. The grave and headstone now had a pipe fence around it. Terry had made a card which reads: "For 128 years this brother in Christ who now rests in Christ has been giving his silent testimony of faith to all who have read this headstone and those to whom it has been told. I wonder how many will share his rest through his testimony." The headstone reads,

Joseph Alexander McPharlin
Died 10th Jan 1883 Aged 25

"Blessed are they that die in the Lord." R.I.P.

> Fear not my friends, my time has come,
>   Oh happy is the day.
> Christ with His precious blood has been
>   and washed my sins away.
> Our happiness shall be complete
>   When we meet beyond the sky.
> We shall never have to part again
>   Or ever say goodbye.

Innisfail and Babinda

I THINK I was in my second year at college when I was posted to a place called Innisfail in far north Queensland for three month's summer relief work. I was to look after the Presbyterian churches at Innisfail and also Babinda, a much smaller town north of Innisfail. We drove north the 1,600 kilometres from Brisbane to Innisfail (which is about 100 kilometres south of Cairns, Babinda being about 60).

My family lapped up the tropical weather. My mother-in-law, Margaret Notini, came up by train to visit. She loved it too. We were able to spend some free time at the beach, swimming in the Pacific. The downside were the "stingers" in the water – which were mostly bluebottle jellyfish. However, the local council erected large nets in an effort to protect swimmers.

As I floated peacefully in the water admiring the bright and pleasant surroundings, I couldn't help but think how wonderful is the Creator of all these things: glimmering sandy beaches, palm trees, and the turquoise ocean. Isn't this the earthly "utopia" I had wished for when I was shovelling snow back in "Winterpeg," Manitoba? I suppose splashing Pacific water on myself was one way of keeping cool under the glow of a glorious tropical sun! The sparkling beach sand was bleached white, and mango trees – branches breaking under the weight of their fat, juicy fruit – were more plentiful than palm trees!

At theological college, I had learned that although God reveals Himself through the things He has made – such as the enticing tropical scene I was viewing through my cheap sunglasses – the spectacles of His written Word are needed for us to see Him properly. John Calvin, likening the Bible to eyeglasses, is saying that everything about God remains fuzzy without the aid of God's Word to clarify truth.

As I lapped up the good life on my summer break in far-north Queensland, I wondered if what I was seeing was anything like the Paradise of old. Mind you, when Adam ate the forbidden fruit in the Garden of Eden, he sinned against God. And the Bible says that sin is the transgression of God's Law (summarized in the Ten Commandments). But it's a comforting thing to know that when God made us, He engraved His Commandments in positive form upon our hearts. For this means that each of us, in our own conscience, knows that it is wrong to steal, commit adultery, lie, etc.

Viewed through the "glasses" of God's Word, the golden sands, palm trees, and turquoise ocean reveal something of the beauty of the Creator reflected in His creation. The bluebottle jellyfish? They remind us that something is not quite right with our present "paradise." Why do these stingers have to spoil a pleasant day at the beach? If we ask this question, we have to go all the way and ask why death has to spoil life for us? Why is there pain, suffering, and death in creation?

In my studies, I learned that the Bible teaches that the wages of sin is death. This means that Adam's sin – and our own sinful disposition which is inborn in each of us – accounts for the sin and misery we see in the world around us. Pain, suffering, and death do not reflect the nature of God, rather they reflect the consequences of our fallen nature, which is part of God's judgment upon our sin. God created mankind perfect and placed us in a perfect Paradise in the beginning, but like starlings fouling their own nests, so we (in Adam) destroyed our own habitat. But worse than this, according to the Bible, we also destroyed ourselves.

Directly behind its pulpit, the church at Babinda has a visual reminder of the perfect nature of God and the fallen nature of man. Behind the place where the preacher stands is a huge block of wood with the Ten Commandments engraved upon it. The eyes of the congregation are forced to look at those commandments each Lord's Day while at worship.

Members of the congregation showed me photographs of the time during the 1980s when a cyclone hit their little paradise – a reminder of the power of God. The church building was levelled and everything demolished. The only object left standing was the wooden block with the Ten Commandments! One is reminded of the Scripture: "All flesh is grass, and its loveliness is like the flower of the field. The grass withers, the flower fades, because the breath of the LORD blows upon it; but surely people are grass. The grass withers, the flower fades, but the word of our God stands forever" (Isa. 40:6–8).

One might wonder why God destroyed His house of worship at Babinda. It just goes to prove that God causes the sun to shine and rain to fall on both the just and the unjust (Matthew 5:45b). In other words, Christians are not exempt from pain, suffering, and death in this life. However, according to the Bible, God does take fallen human beings, regenerates them, replaces their dead hearts with new ones, rewrites His Law on these new fleshly tablets, and begins to rebuild their lives. Though their bodies crumble back to dust at death, their reborn souls (with the Word of God written on their hearts) remain standing before God, even the judgment of God. Then comes a period of rebuilding when finally the Christian's body will be resurrected and reunited with his soul at the Last Day.

Just as "in the beginning," the Triune God created the heavens and the earth and all that is in them, so "at the end" (i.e., at the new beginning), the Triune God will create all things new again. Therefore, this fallen and sin-pocked world will be completely renewed at some future point in time. "And God will wipe away every tear from their eyes; there shall be no more death, nor sorrow, nor crying. There shall be no more pain, for the former things have passed away. Then He who sat on the throne said, 'Behold, I make all things new.' And He said to me, 'Write, for these words are true and faithful'" (Rev. 21:4–5a).

Cyclone Larry demolished 80 percent of Innisfail and just about all of Babinda in 2006, but that which was destroyed has been renewed.

> 2) O tell of His might, O sing of His grace,
>   Whose robe is the light, whose canopy space.
>   His chariots of wrath the deep thunderclouds form,
>   And dark is His path on the wings of the storm.
>
> — Robert Grant (1779–1838)
> Hymn 9, RCH

Seeing through New Eyes

J COULD see in the Bible that Jesus encourages us to study God's creation for illustrations and revelation of the ways that God cares for His creatures. Through studying the Bible, I have developed a new life and worldview. I began to see the world through new eyes.

Jesus says, "Therefore I say to you, do not worry about your life, what you will eat or what you will drink; nor about your body, what you will put on. Is life not more than food and the body more than clothing?" (Matt. 6:25). Thus there is more to life than eating, drinking, and making merry. But this is not to say that there is anything wrong with eating, drinking, or making merry, for the Bible is replete with examples of God blessing His people in Old Testament times with an abundance of food and drink, and even describes the Promised Land in terms of milk and honey with hills dripping with wine.

I used to believe that Christians were killjoys. When I was growing up in Scotland, John Knox and John Calvin were portrayed as "the terrible twins" who tried to stamp out all the last vestiges of fun! But that impression has changed for me. Now, Calvin speaks for me when he says, "Nor was it ever forbidden to laugh, or to be full, or to add new to old and hereditary possessions, or to be delighted with music, or to drink wine" (*Institutes*, Book 3, 19:9, Beverage Translation).

Robert L. Reymond provides a bit of an insight into John Calvin's character. Says Reymond:

> We will conclude this first lecture after I address one final matter about Calvin's youth and young manhood. Adolf von Harnack (1851–1930), the Ritschlian church historian, perniciously described Calvin as "the man who never smiled." This is a very wrong assessment of Calvin's character. Calvin taught that "laughter is the gift of God," and he held it [to be] the right, or rather the duty, of the Christian man to practice it in due season. He is constantly joking with friends in his letters, and he eagerly joins with them in all the joys of life. "I wish I were with you for half a day," he writes to one of them, "to laugh with you...." He enjoyed a joke hugely, with

that open-mouthed laugh, which, as one of his biographers phrases it, belonged to the men of the sixteenth century." (Reymond quotes B. B. Warfield for that last bit. *John Calvin: His Life and Influence*, Christian Focus Publications, 2004, 33)

I came to see that the "good" things in life are reminders of Eden, while at the same time being symbols of the things of Heaven (i.e., the joy of life for all resurrected believers on the New Earth). To me, the beautiful things in this present world are revelation of the face of God. But Henry Van Til offers this caution:

> Simply to behold the beauty in this world does not bring us into a personal relationship with God, although beauty is still the first guide to God. For beauty reveals His attributes of goodness, wisdom, omnipotence, righteousness, and His providential care. Therefore, unbelievers are without excuse since this beauty of God is universally displayed. (*The Calvinistic Concept of Culture*, Baker Books, reprint 2001, 108)

Jesus invites us to look at the things of creation so that we might see an illustration of the beauty and the providential care of God. He says, "Look at the birds of the air, for they neither sow nor reap nor gather into barns; yet your heavenly Father feeds them. Are you not worth more than they?" (Matt. 6:26). By inviting us to consider things of creation, Jesus is alerting us that God is known by analogy.

As a Mason, I had learned about symbolism, i.e., that certain objects may be used to represent other things. As a Minister, I learned that symbols are sometimes simply mini-illustrations of analogies. For example, pomegranates, "from the exuberance of their seeds," may denote plenty. But the pomegranate is also analogous of God, particularly the "one and many" aspect of the God who made it. The fruit itself reflects the Trinity in that it has an outer layer or skin called the exocarp, a middle layer called the mesocarp, and an inner layer called the endocarp. Thus, the pomegranate used by Masons to symbolize "plenty" is also analogous of our Creator *and* Provider.

With the use of analogy in mind, the study of God's creation viewed in the light of His written Word brings knowledge and understanding. It is in creation, and in the events of creation's history, that we may see something of the "Beloved" looking at us "through the lattice." At the time of the Reformation, Calvin was the one who expounded what the Bible says about these things. Henry Van Til explains it thus:

> Calvin thinks of the history of man on earth as cosmic drama, of which God is at the same time author and spectator. Beauty is the divine lustre of glory reflected from the thought and work of God.
>
> There are three acts in this drama: before the fall, in the perfect harmony of heaven and paradise; between the fall and redemption, in which beauty is symbolic – witness the temple of Solomon – and preparation for and expectation of the Messiah is the central theme; finally, in the third period, the glory of the Lord becomes flesh in the Son. And although "He had no form nor comeliness, with no beauty that we should desire Him" (Isa. 53:2), yet there shone forth in Him a spiritual beauty so that "He that hath seen Me hath seen the Father" (John 14:9), and "we beheld His glory, glory as of the only begotten from the Father" (John 1:14).
>
> (The Calvinistic Concept of Culture,
Baker Books, reprint 2001, 108)

My own life and worldview (which is that of "Calvinism") is simply about seeing God's invisible hand in providence, His beautiful face in creation, and hearing His heart beat as we, in a manner of speaking, place our heads upon the breast of His only begotten Son, Jesus Christ. Calvinism is about doing all things to the glory of God, and enjoying His presence even this side of Paradise. In a word, Calvinism is Christianity in its most dynamic form!

> Glory be to God the Father,
> Glory be to God the Son,
> Glory be to God the Spirit,
> Great Jehovah, Three in One!
> Glory, glory,
> While eternal ages run!
>   – Horatius Bonar (1808–1889)
>   Hymn 7, RCH

Compassionate Nature

WHILE in Canada, it had been my prayer that God would gather Dorothy's family together to settle in Brisbane. She and her brother Alan were now together again. Next came her sister Elizabeth with her husband Robert. Then, before we knew it, her mother Margaret had arrived. Prayers answered!

Robert had an old Norton Commando motorcycle, brought with him from Scotland. I never really liked motorbikes. Dangerous things, I thought. However, Robert managed to coax me into riding pillion. Off we would go up among the cool slopes of Mount Glorious and Mount Nebo, stopping off at small towns such as Dayboro, Samford, and Samsonvale for lunch and what have you along the way. Queensland is beautiful. In the woods, the volume of noise made by the individual cicada beetle, multiplied by the many trillions of its siblings and cousins, might equal that of the "Hamden roar" when Scotland scores against England!

One time Robert stopped the motorcycle on a road running beside what looked like a fairly dried-up creek. After saying, "Watch this," he proceeded to gently lift a boulder. It was like he was visiting an old friend. I looked down and there was a yabby* looking up at us. It was landlocked in a pool that was nearly evaporated. Robert picked up and carried the thirsty little critter to where it could go downstream into a bigger pool – hoping that some big fish or other wouldn't fancy his wee friend for lunch!

Some would say that this is interfering with "nature," that nature should be allowed to take its own course. But this is to fail to see that man is part of nature, too. For what is "unnatural" about man? Man is part of that giant machinery we call nature. The whole of creation is the machine, and the machine has many working components. The Triune God made the yabby. God made man. God made nature. To leave a creature to die for no other reason than to allow "nature" to take its course is to deify nature! It is to grant the decree of life and death to nature.

---

* Yabby: A small, Australian crayfish.

And who is to say that Robert and I were not directed to that yabby by God so as to preserve that little creature, alive, at least for a while longer? Yes, nature – that is to say "fallen nature" – might be red in tooth and claw, but that doesn't mean we have to be! Nor does it mean the we are not part of nature. It simply means that, like our Creator, we have the ability to express mercy and compassion. To be sure, though well-meaning in our wish to preserve, we may at times do more harm than good; nevertheless, we have the desire and ability to show mercy and compassion.

Wasn't it an act of mercy and compassion by God when He sent His only begotten Son into the world to rescue fallen creatures by going to the cross in their place? Was the yabby rescue not an ever-so-faint reflection – whether symbolic or analogous – of God's own grace toward us?

> 1) When I survey the wondrous cross
>   On which the Prince of Glory died,
>   My richest gain I count but loss,
>   And pour contempt on all my pride.
>
> 4) Were the whole realm of Nature mine,
>   That were an offering far too small;
>   Love so amazing, so divine,
>   Demands my soul, my life, my all.
>
> — Isaac Watts (1674–1748)
> Hymn 106, RCH

Christian Liberty

IT was John Calvin at the time of the Reformation who liberated the whole realm of culture from the tutelage of the church. At that time, "nature" and "grace" were viewed as existing in separate spheres. In simple terms, nature was held to belong to the realm "downstairs" (of the earth) and grace pertained to things "upstairs" (or of the heavenly realm). And if reason relates to nature, and faith to grace, then reason and faith also exist in separate spheres. Today, this has degenerated into a false dichotomy between "science" and "faith."

It is supposed that faith deals with the supernatural, while science with natural things, or, to put it another way, it is supposed by some that religion deals in faith while science deals with fact. Viewed strictly within these terms, it is easy to see why I had grown up in two minds! God, angels, salvation – what Christians believe – all belong to the faith realm, and faith is the place where things cannot be tested in a laboratory. Birds, trees, animals, plants, fish, rocks, the sun, the moon, the stars all belong to the realm of reason, i.e., science, and can be studied in a laboratory. On account of this sort of faulty reasoning, it is therefore thought (by some) that Christian faith and science are incompatible.

Calvinism is distinctive in its outright rejection of this reasoning. Calvinism teaches that it is faulty because this type of thought presupposes human autonomy from the God who created us. In other words, Calvinists believe that we must begin all our studies, all our observations of anything – be it God, angels, miracles, birds, trees, pomegranates, bees, geology, mathematics, geometry, etc., etc. – with God, and not man. The true Biblical view is fully God-centred, while other "isms" – be they religious or nonreligious – are Man-centred, and, as such, will fail to fully apprehend the true nature of things. God speaking in His Word are the glasses mankind must wear, and is the only way of true scientific study, no matter the field.

Calvin was one of the main initiators of the great social liberty we now enjoy in the West (in places such as Scotland, Canada, Australia, and America), for Calvin rejected as unbiblical the view that grace and faith have only to do with ethics, religion, theology, and the church, while nature and reason have to do with the things of culture, i.e., those natural things that men do. By rejecting this view, Calvin, from his study of the Bible, freed Western society from the interference of church legislation that essentially forbade freedom of thought and expression.

The church at that time had been massively and pervasively under the influence of the ancient pagan Greek philosopher, Aristotle. Thus Calvin, by his reasoning based upon God speaking in Scripture, enabled both church and state (and the people who belong to these overlapping spheres) to likewise start thinking in terms of God and His truth, and not the pagan Aristotelian philosophy that had stifled cultural growth for centuries. Calvin believed that the church and state should remain distinct and serve God in their respective spheres. John Knox applied this Biblical principle in Scotland and that nation soon after became (for a time) one of the greatest places of learning in the world. The same Biblical principle was imported to colonial America.

Since the time of Calvin and the Reformation, there have been many periods when even whole nations have lapsed back into the imaginary – and therefore false – dichotomy between faith and reason. Evolutionism and Marxism are two belief-systems or philosophies – or "isms" – we have already talked about. If it is not a corrupt church that suppresses the people, it is a corrupt state such as those under the dominating influence of Marxism or evolutionism. Sometimes it's both at the same time!

Calvin had a Biblical "safety-device" to help prevent this while encouraging cultural advancement. It had a Greek name: *adiaphora*. Henry van Til explains it for us:

> William of Occam, the nominalist philosopher, in opposing this overlordship [i.e., the placing of the whole sphere of culture under the tutelage of the church so that it becomes the handmaid of theology], sets the two realms over against each other antithetically. He, indeed, would deliver art and agriculture, commerce and trade from the power of the pope, but he turns it over to the dukes and kings. Thus he became the father of a state-controlled culture, the first modern philosopher of totalitarianism.
>
> Now Calvin proclaimed alongside the church and state a third realm, an area of life that has a separate existence and jurisdiction. It is called the sphere of the adiaphora, the things indifferent. This is the court of conscience. No king or

pope may here hold sway. This area is not restricted to a few insignificant matters of taste and opinion among individuals, but it includes music, architecture, technical learning, science, social festivities, and the everyday questions, "what shall we eat and what shall we drink and where-withal shall we be clothed?" Now Calvin proclaims freedom from both church and state for this whole large area of life in his doctrine of Christian liberty, making man responsible and accountable to God alone for his conscience. This doctrine of Christian liberty is therefore one of the foundation stones of Calvin's cultural philosophy. (*The Calvinistic Concept of Culture*, Baker Books, reprint 2001, 99)

Perhaps paradoxically, the "Christian liberty" spoken of here is about the Christian "bringing every thought into captivity to the obedience of Christ" (2 Cor. 10:5b). Therefore, if the Christian wishes to be obedient to Christ in music, architecture, technical learning, science, social festivities, eating, drinking, and wearing clothes, etc., he needs to search the Scriptures to find out how God may best be glorified in the area of adiaphora (1 Cor. 10:31). Although the church and the state, each in its respective sphere of authority, ought to encourage the good and discourage the bad even in our cultural activities, each individual conscience ought to be bound by nothing other than God speaking by His Spirit in His Word.

They Builded Better Than They Knew

THE Apostle Paul, under inspiration of the Holy Spirit, says, "According to the grace of God which was given to me, as a wise master builder I have laid the foundation, and another builds on it. But let each one take heed how he builds on it. For no other foundation can anyone lay than that which is laid, which is Jesus Christ" (1 Cor. 3:10–11). According to the grace of God, John Calvin built upon this foundation. And, according to the grace of God, the Calvinist Christians who followed him continued building upon the sure foundation that is Jesus Christ.

The grace of God in Jesus Christ is the keystone that supports the triumphal rainbow-archway through which all Christian enterprise marches. Because Calvinism interprets the Bible to mean we are to implicitly trust in the sovereign God's grace alone for our salvation from everlasting judgment, I believe that Christians are free from the stultifying bondage of always and ever trying to please God in order to gain entrance into His kingdom. Thus, as a Christian, I found I had liberty of conscience and was now free to take every thought into the captivity of obedience to Christ. To be sure this is not to say that I and other Christians never entertain a sinful thought, but it is to say that Christians are no longer in bondage to sin. Set free from always wondering if we have done enough to please God, Christians are then able to consider and delight in the deep things of God.

Jesus asks us to look at the birds of the air and also says, "Consider the lilies of the field, how they grow: they neither toil nor spin; and yet I say to you that even Solomon in all his glory was not arrayed like one of these. Now if God so clothes the grass of the field, which today is, and tomorrow is thrown into the oven, will He not much more clothe you, O you of little faith? Therefore do not worry, saying, 'What shall we eat?' or 'What shall we drink?' or 'What shall we wear?' For after all these things the Gentiles seek. For your heavenly Father knows that you need all these things. But seek first the kingdom of God and His righteousness, and all these things will be added to you. Therefore do not worry about tomorrow, for tomorrow will worry about its own things. Sufficient for the day is its own trouble" (Matt. 6:28–34).

The Christian according to Calvinism has freedom in every sphere of life because he seeks first the kingdom of God and His righteousness in *every* sphere of life. Masonry seeks to take a good man and make him better. Calvinist Christianity can take whole societies, even whole nations, and make them better.

Christ is made the sure foundation,
Christ the head and corner-stone,
Chosen by the Lord, and precious,
Binding all the Church in one,
Holy Zion's help forever,
And her confidence alone.

— Latin, 7th or 8th century
Translation by John Mason Neale
Hymn 207, RCH

Minister Meets Mason

As a Christian minister, am I at liberty to meet the Mason on the level? Or do I now see myself so high above everyone that I have to condescend from a very great height to meet with them? Only Christ – the "Bread of Heaven" – has such an exalted position, yet He meets with sinners such as ministers and Masons. As a sinner saved by God's grace alone, in the words of a preacher, I am merely one beggar telling other beggars where to find bread!

The Mason meets others "on the level" on account of his belief that all men are created equal, and that religions are equal. But as I moved from being a Mason to being a minister, so did my "foundation" for meeting people on the level. Now God's grace, and God's grace alone, is the reason I am able to meet all others on the level regardless of their station and vocation in life. As God is gracious toward me, so I ought to be gracious to others. This is true Christian humility. It is to practice loving God and your neighbour as yourself, which is to image the triune God.

While participating in Freemasonry, it was my personal observation and experience that most Masons were content to own only a general knowledge of Freemasonry, leaving the particulars to be observed by a more zealous minority. To be sure, all Masons are privy to what goes on behind the wall of a Masonic lodge at work, but what message or messages are those rituals conducted therein really trying to convey?

If Masonry teaches its members a general morality summed up in Faith, Hope, and Charity, then what are some of the "particulars" that make up this "general" morality? Faith in God, Hope in salvation, and Charity to all men is a good summary of what Masons hold dear. But what principle in the first instance makes Faith, Hope, and Charity general virtues that all men ought to practice for the betterment of mankind? What undergirds it? What is the heart of Masonic teaching, and why? Is it just good to be good? If so, how is "good" defined? What is Masonry really trying to achieve?

I touched on this earlier, but as a Mason I was taught that Freemasonry is a "beautiful system of morality, veiled in allegory, and illustrated by symbols." Later, I could see a correlation between this and what I began learning as I was training to be a minister. For while training for the ministry, I began to learn of Old Testament "types" and their New Testament "anti-types." In other words, while persons in the Old Testament (Adam, Noah, Abraham, David, Solomon, etc.) are real human beings with flaws like the rest of us, their persons, characters, and historical situations and environments, on many occasions, are also symbolic of people and events that have come, and are coming to pass in New Testament times (which includes our own day). The New Testament itself records some fulfillment.

Simply put, I see certain similarities between, on the one hand, the "morality plays" acted out in each of the Masonic degrees (with their attending lectures) and, on the other hand, the historical narration of people and events recorded in the Old Testament. Indeed, good morals are taught in and by both simply because the Old Testament Scriptures are used in Blue Lodge Masonry. But, for example, look at King Solomon arrayed in all his splendour. Is the reign of Solomon not more than an example of good rulership? And is the Temple he built not more than an example of good craftsmanship? For when one reads the New Testament, one finds that these real and historical people, events, and objects are, at the same time, prophetic symbols or predictive illustrations. They are living analogies of things far greater than themselves!

Are we not able to see then, even by way of this simple observation, that the general morals taught in the Masonic lodge and in the Old Testament – as valuable as these might be – are simply a series of individual or "particular" pillars supporting a much larger "general" platform? The general morals presented in Masonry and the Old Testament simply reflect the Triune God in that they reveal, just as in the Godhead, that there are many aspects to the one.

The principle I'm trying to address might be summarized in a variation of an old adage: Some cannot see the trees for the forest, but others cannot see the forest for the trees! The ability to see both is the implied desire. Additionally, one must look above the treetops to see the source of the light that allows us to see both the forest *and* the trees. But the sun is not the ultimate source of light – God is. Since Satan is an angel of darkness who poses as an angel of light, great discernment is needed to distinguish that which is truly good from that which merely seems good. As the Scripture teaches, "Your Word is a lamp to my feet and a light to my path" (Ps. 119:105), and "There is a way that *seems* right to a man, but its end is the way of death" (Prov. 16:25, *emphasis mine*).

1) Be Thou my Vision, O Lord of my heart;
   Naught be all else to me, save that Thou art,
   Thou my best thought, by day or by night,
   Waking or sleeping, Thy presence my light.

3) High King of heaven, after victory won,
   May I reach heaven's joys, O bright heaven's Sun!
   Heart of my own heart, whatever befall,
   Still be my Vision, O Ruler of all.

Ancient Irish, translation by Mary Byrne (1880–1931)
Versified by Eleanor Hull (1860–1935)
Hymn 477, RCH

Dad's Funeral

ONE of the disadvantages of living overseas is the tyranny of distance. My three daughters grew up without really getting to know my mum and dad. Jennifer had met my mum and dad when she was 2 years old when we were back in Scotland on a month's holiday from Canada. Nina went back with me from Australia for a month when she was 14. She never got to meet my mum who had passed away back in 1989. And poor Fionna never met my mum and dad at all.

I was living in Tasmania in November 2005 when I was notified that my dad had been taken to the Gartnavel General Hospital in Glasgow. He was 83, very ill, and not expected to live much longer. He was surprisingly lucid when I entered his single-room ward in the hospital. As he saw me, his face lit up and he said, "Neil! You've come all the way from Tasmania just to see me!" He said this as if he thought it strange that I would waste my time coming to see someone as insignificant as my own father! I had missed being by my mother's side when she died at age 57. I was determined I would be there for Dad.

I stayed with my sister Catriona and her husband Neil and their two children Katie and Hamish. I was at the hospital daily to see Dad who was deteriorating quickly. Catriona and my brother Stuart lived relatively close to the hospital, but my other siblings, Mhairi and Fearghas, lived too far away to commute daily, but visited whenever they could.

Apparently my dad was dying of old age and not the cancerous tumour in his lower bowel. This "old age" condition presented a problem with the hospice we had hoped to get Dad into for the special care and attention that general hospitals are not able to give. Even though my dad was definitely dying, technically Dad couldn't be admitted to the hospice unless he had a terminal illness!

I was in Scotland a fortnight before my dad (after much deliberation) was permitted to enter St. Margaret's Hospice in Clydebank.

The Gartnavel Hospital was to notify us when they were about to move my dad to the hospice. It was on a Friday when Catriona's phone rang and we were informed that my dad was being moved to the hospice sometime after lunch. It was suggested that we give him time to get settled in before visiting that evening.

The phone rang at 4:40 that evening. We were told to come quickly, that our dad had taken a turn for the worse. Clock ticking, we made for the hospice in Clydebank with great haste. As the two of us drove toward the Erskine Bridge with Catriona at the wheel, we decided to use the mobile phone to alert our sister and brothers to Dad's situation. Stuart would meet us at the hospice. Catriona and I arrived first. We were asked to wait in the foyer. We were told someone would come and get us. It was when we were invited to enter a sitting room that I began to realize that we had arrived too late. A compassionate nun with a soothing Irish accent gently broke the news to us. Did we want to see our dad?

He looked peaceful enough as he lay there with his arms folded on his chest like a St. Andrew's Cross. He was wearing a big watch on his skinny left wrist. In the quiet and still room, the ticking of its second hand caught my attention. It began to slightly agitate me. It seemed disrespectful that the watch would keep on ticking like nothing had happened when my dad had just died! Why hadn't it stopped ticking when my dad's heart had stopped beating?

At our dead father's side, Catriona and I comforted each other with a long sibling embrace. Then came the tears. As we waited for Stuart to arrive, I phoned Fearghas and Mhairi. I estimated that our dad had died somewhere between 4:40 and 4:45 p.m. After travelling all the way from Tasmania to be by his side, I had missed his passing by half an hour! Stuart arrived at the hospice and I told him the news as we walked up a stairway. Stuart went into the room to see Dad.

The three of us went back to Catriona's place. We were kind of quiet. I began to study the painting hanging on the wall. It was another one of Fearghas' early works. It depicts a geranium growing out of a terra-cotta pot. There is also a Bible in the painting. I could tell by the writing on the side of it that it was a Bible Fearghas had given to Dad many years ago. The painting was getting close to forty years old. I recognized another object in the painting sitting on top of my dad's Bible. It was the old alarm clock (with luminous hands) that we had when we were younger. I commented to Stuart and Catriona about the Bible being Dad's Bible. But then I said, "Look at the time on the clock." Its hands were depicting the exact time I had estimated Dad had died! I was comforted by the knowledge that even the very moment of my dad's death was in accordance with the providence of the God who works all things together for good.

I extended my stay in Scotland so that I could attend the funeral. The Rev. Ian Miller had another funeral to attend to, but he allowed us to use his Bonhill Parish Church on the River Leven where I conducted the funeral service with many relatives and friends in attendance. My brother Stuart gave a eulogy. Fearghas read a poem he had written about my dad and Stuart. My niece, Cara (Fearghas' daughter) sang a beautiful and comforting solo about the depth of God's love for us.

I mentioned to the Rev. Ian Miller that the last time I had attended his church was when I was working on its leaky roof as a plumber's apprentice. I remember it being a hot summer that year and swimming in the River Leven to cool off at lunchtime. Who would have thought that I would have been back in it thirty years later preaching the Gospel to old friends and relatives! God is gracious!

God's Covenant of Peace

DON'T know about you, but when I see trees I tend to think of the Garden of Eden. It is interesting to note that in the Bible the word *eden* means "pleasure" or "delight." Eden is Paradise, which is a real picture of Heaven, the place of bliss. After the Triune God created and made the heavens and the earth, the sea, and all that is in them, He created man in His own image. The following verse details how God formed man: "And the Lord God formed man of the dust of the ground, and breathed into his nostrils the breath of life; and man became a living being. The Lord God planted a garden eastward in Eden, and there He put the man whom He had formed" (Gen. 2:7–8).

Note that Eden's Garden was east in Eden. Masonry holds that light is knowledge. In a Masonic lodge the light (i.e., knowledge) comes from the Worshipful Master who sits in the "East" and spreads throughout the lodge, just as the sun (from man's perspective) rises in the east, runs its course across the face of the whole earth, and sets in the west. The Garden of Eden in the east (of Eden) is the centre of knowledge.

Note what the Bible says next: "And out of the ground the Lord God made every tree grow that is pleasant to the sight and good for food. The tree of life was also in the midst of the garden, and the tree of the knowledge of good and evil" (Gen. 2:9). The tree of knowledge is not just a tree of knowledge, per se, but is the tree of the knowledge of "good and evil." Therefore, there is a moral dimension to this tree. That moral dimension is spelt out in the following verses: "Then the Lord God took the man and put him in the garden to tend and keep it. And the Lord God commanded the man, saying, 'Of every tree in the garden you may freely eat; but of the tree of the knowledge of good and evil you shall not eat, for in the day that you eat of it you shall surely die'" (Gen. 2:15–17).

The tree, then, doesn't necessarily need to have any material qualities that make it different from other trees. Rather, we see that it is the command of God to man that makes this tree a special tree. That command comes from a place above the treetops. It comes from God in Heaven, of which the Edenic Paradise is a reflective picture. Freemasonry acknowledges God as the source of all morals, and therefore, that God is the source of all true knowledge, teaching that good morals are based on accurate knowledge of good and evil. Just as there is in the centre of the Masonic lodge an altar with the Volume of the Sacred Law (i.e., God's Word) laying open upon it, men kneeling before it, and a letter "G" (representing God) hanging above it, so the tree of life and the tree of the knowledge of good and evil are in the centre of the Garden of Eden, beside which were Adam and Eve (who had God's Moral and Sacred Law written on their hearts), and God looking down from above. In Solomon's Temple, the Ark of the Covenant resided in the Holy of Holies. The Ark was essentially an altar. Inside the box of the Ark was the Covenant Law, i.e., the Ten Commandments, which Moral Law man had broken. Above the Ark was the God who dwelt between the cherubim whose faces were looking down on the Ark from above.

Notice that not only was man (as federally represented by Adam) supposed to keep, as a test, God's outward and verbal command to refrain from eating the fruit of the tree of the knowledge of good and evil (which meant that man was to keep the Ten Commandments written on his heart by God at his creation), but God had commissioned man to tend and keep His garden. Here the word "tend" means to cultivate, and the word "keep" means guard. Adam was to cultivate the Garden of Eden as well as guard it. Thus man was employed by God to work for God in God's garden.

As an employer might try out a new employee for a probationary period before granting him full wages and fulltime employment, so God covenanted with Adam as head of the human race. If Adam remained obedient to God – i.e., if Adam perfectly kept all God's commandments while tending and keeping the garden – then God would reward his obedience and labour. This was the covenant or contract that God graciously entered into with Adam. All present-day social contracts have their foundations in man's obedience to God and His Law in Eden.

It is perhaps redundant to say that law and its enforcement are for keeping peace. As long as Adam kept God's covenant, man had peace with God and with his neighbour. Thus peace begins and ends with God. There are three historically real places where this peace is exemplified: Eden's Garden, Solomon's Temple, and Christ's Kingdom which is the kingdom of Heaven. The first two typify the third.

Eden's Garden

IT was in the garden – the garden God had planted eastward in Eden – that a major drama that affected the whole of creation was acted out. We learn a great deal from this action-drama as recorded in the Bible – much more than anything that could ever be acted out in a Masonic lodge. In this high drama, there was a man, a woman, a tree, a serpent, and the LORD God. The LORD God had made the woman from Adam's own rib. She was bone of his bones, and flesh of his flesh. She was his wife, and she was to be his helper in the Garden.

The Lord God issued to the man and the woman, Adam and Eve (and all mankind through them), the "Cultural Mandate." The Cultural Mandate is summarized in the following where the Triune God said, "'Let Us make man in Our image, according to Our likeness; let them have dominion over the fish of the sea, over the birds of the air, and over the cattle, over all the earth and over every creeping thing that creeps on the earth.' So God created man in His own image; in the image of God He created him; male and female He created them. Then God blessed them, and God said to them, 'Be fruitful and multiply; fill the earth and subdue it; have dominion over the fish of the sea, over the birds of the air, and over every living thing that moves on the earth'" (Gen. 1:26–28).

God had gone all out for the happy couple by placing them in a literal paradise where they were instructed to obediently "go to it." To them, the work God had assigned was not a sludge of drudge! Rather, everything they did was a delight – an "Eden" – to them because everything they did, they did to the glory of the Maker of all things. This was no Marxist, Buddhist, or any other type of wished-for utopia. This was the real thing! But in the garden, at a certain point in time, the drama intensified – and something terrible happened.

The drama centred round a single tree, the tree of the knowledge of good and evil, which was literally in the centre of the garden. "The tree of life was also in the midst of the garden, and the tree of the knowledge of good and evil" (Genesis 2:9). How did Adam know which of all the trees was the tree of the knowledge of good and evil? Presumably God had shown Adam the particular tree and he had, in turn, told Eve which one it was. Because of the covenant God had made with Adam, the whole future of mankind was tied up in what Adam would do with the fruit of this tree. This was the outward test of the covenant.

Keeping in mind that the man was commissioned by God to cultivate and guard the garden, we are alerted to something very significant. Adam knew the properties of every tree and every animal in the garden. God had brought every beast of the field and every bird to Adam to see what he would name them: "So Adam gave names to all cattle, to the birds of the air, and to every beast of the field" (Genesis 2:20a). Assigning names to the animals and birds means that Adam knew or had intimate knowledge of the animals' very being. He knew what they were and he named them accordingly. As a super-scientist with great spiritual insight, he knew what made each living thing tick. But more than that, he could see the revelation of God in the things God had made. Every animal, bird, plant, shrub, and tree, typified or reflected some attribute or aspect of its Maker.

In the garden there was only peace and harmony between the man and wife, man and beast, and flora and fauna. All creation reflected the peace and harmony of the Triune Godhead who had said, "Let Us make man in Our image." Thus, peace and harmony are aspects of the image of God.

Part of the Cultural Mandate is the cultivation of the initial peace and harmony that has its very foundation in the Godhead. As man's representative before God, for Adam to break the covenant with the Godhead was to also break the harmony God had built into His creation. When Adam ate the forbidden fruit, God cursed the ground on account of man. Thus disharmony entered all of creation through Adam's sin: "Then to Adam He said, 'Because you have heeded the voice of your wife, and have eaten from the tree of which I commanded you, saying, "You shall not eat of it": Cursed is the ground for your sake; in toil you shall eat of it all the days of your life. Both thorns and thistles it shall bring forth for you, and you shall eat the herb of the field. In the sweat of your face you shall eat bread till you return to the ground, for out of it you were taken; for dust you are, and to dust you shall return' " (Gen. 3:17–19).

In light of this, it is clear that the utopian dreams of Karl Marx and others can never be realized. Which is to say that there can be no "return to Eden" for Karl Marx or any of his followers. For Marx took no account of the fall of man when he compiled his version of dialectical materialism. Therefore, his utopian dream of a Marxist state can never be realized because the "material" of Marx's dialectical materialism belongs to God, not man! Also, it is not "work" that is cursed, but rather the ground, i.e., the worker's material! But more than that, after Adam broke the covenant, there was now disharmony between the man and the woman. For Adam blamed his wife for his demise: "The woman that You put here with me – she gave me the fruit and I ate it" (Genesis 3:12). And did you notice that he also blamed God! – "the woman that *You* put here with me" (*emphasis mine*).

So, not only was there disharmony between man and the creation in which he dwelt, there was disharmony between a man and his wife – and, ultimately, between all human beings. But there was also disharmony between mankind and their Maker. And if that isn't bad enough, each human being is in disharmony with himself! For after Adam and Eve had eaten the fruit of the tree of the knowledge of good and evil they both learned something they didn't know before: "They knew that they were naked; and they sewed fig leaves together, and made themselves aprons. . . . and hid themselves from the presence of the LORD God amongst the trees of the garden" (Gen. 3:7–8, KJV). By covering themselves, Adam and Eve revealed they had received an accusing conscience.

But the LORD God is gracious. We read of Him clothing the naked Adam and Eve with proper aprons. "Unto Adam also and to his wife did the LORD God make coats of skin, and clothed them" (Gen. 3:21). The Masonic apron is made of lambskin. Presumably, before the watching eyes of Adam and Eve, the LORD God shed the blood of a lamb – sacrificed it – and used its skin to give them proper covering. This act symbolizes that Great Sacrifice, to which all the Old Testament sacrifices pointed, i.e., the crucifixion of the Lamb of God who takes away the sin of the world and clothes Christians with His own righteousness.

And in His loving kindness, Adam and Eve were expelled from the Garden. "So He drove out the man: and He placed cherubim at the east of the garden of Eden, and a flaming sword which turned every way, to guard the way to the tree of life" (Gen. 3:24).

Turning Fifty

$\mathcal{G}$ROWING older is a funny thing only when you notice it happening. I'm not a great fan of decimals, but I seem to notice how much the aging process has affected me at the end of each decade of my life. I didn't mind at all when I turned 10, for then I was old enough and ready to play for the Levenvale Primary School football (soccer) team. When I was back in Scotland in 2005 (for my dad's funeral), I even visited my old school and was pleased to see that they still had a photo of the team with yours truly in it. I wish I had smiled in that photo – and that I still had that head of jet-black hair!

When I turned 20, I was ready to take off on my new adventure and return to Ontario, Canada, the place of my birth. I was still fit and healthy then. The Loch Lomond Rowing Club greatly assisted me in attaining and maintaining this state of health. Mind you, I was never one of those guys with bulging muscles that you see on the front of packets of porridge oats. I suppose when I was 20, as to physique, I was somewhere between Olive Oyl and Popeye!

On my 30th birthday, I opened up the curtains on the morning of September 5 and read the long poster some friends had tied to the backyard fence of our Winnipeg home: *HAPPY 30TH BIRTHDAY NEIL!* I remember being in a bit of a flap about turning 30. I thought 30 was, well, quite elderly! Mind you, I was then playing football (soccer) every Saturday each summer for Liverpool – an obviously predominantly scouser* team in Winnipeg. It took me a while before I began to understand the Liverpudlian accent and the more I learned to understand the accent, the more I began to pass the ball! It's weird, but I still find it hard to understand English spoken by many English people!

I turned 40 in the Outback of Australia. We lived in a place called Springsure, in Queensland, a 40-minute drive due south of a fairly large mining town called Emerald. Emerald was right on the Tropic of Capricorn along which the Capricorn Highway runs from Rockhampton on the east coast. The black hair was still as thick as it was when I was 20; however, it was getting a bit frosty. At Springsure as I tended to the congregation, I learned a bit about roping steers, dehorning them, growing crops, weather gauges, and that sort of thing.

Also, Springsure has a 9-hole golf course at the foot of Virgin Rock.** The course was quite rocky on account of rocks falling off and rolling down from Virgin Rock. The first time I tackled Springsure golf course, I twisted my back teeing off at the first tee and was laid up for three days! Virgin Rock has a little alcove, or grotto formation, on its face. Apparently, if you look very carefully, you are able to just make out the shape of the Virgin with Child in the alcove! I'm afraid, not being Roman Catholic, it all looked like just so much rock to me!

Turning 50 was earth-shattering for me. It was then that I started to get a true perspective on time. Fifty years is not long at all! Things that happened a hundred years ago were only five decades beyond my own five! From this perspective, two hundred years is nothing! A thousand years? That's only twenty times fifty!

It's only every time I get a haircut that I'm reminded that there's a great deal of "snow on the ben." As I sit there on the chair, I wonder where all the white-hair clippings are coming from, because, in my own mind, I've still got jet-black hair. In my own mind, I'm still about 25! I suppose in reality, I'm reminded that I'm not 25 every

* Scouser: a native or inhabitant of Liverpool, England.

** Virgin Rock, which is situated on the eastern side of Mount Zamia, has a naturally formed likeness to the Virgin Mary and Child.

morning when I get out of bed. New mattresses never seem to solve the problem of the aches of age!

When I turned 50, I felt as if I should now, at last, start acting my age – but I'm confused; for all I hear is that 70 is the new 40, and 50 is the new 30, and all that sort of thing! Oh well, it's still great to be alive, no matter what age I'm supposed to be!

Solomon's Temple

THE portable Tabernacle used by Israel during the wilderness years was the forerunner of the more permanent Solomon's Temple. Like the Tabernacle before it, the plans for building Solomon's Temple were given by direct revelation of God (see 1 Chron. 28:9-19). Even the Ark of the Covenant that sat in the Holy of Holies was crafted according to revelatory instruction. The building of Solomon's Temple – and everything to do with it – was done to the glory of God. This is what we are calling "Calvinism"! Thus Calvinism in action is the exemplification of the principle of "letting the saw do the work," whereby men work with, rather than against, the laws of God to His glory.

As the Garden was eastward in Eden, so the temple was on the east side of old Jerusalem. The walled city of Jerusalem was an extension of Solomon's Temple. Jerusalem and its temple was a representation of the garden expanded in Eden and developed. As mentioned earlier, "The inside of the temple was cedar, carved with ornamental buds and open flowers. All was cedar; there was no stone to be seen" (1 Ki. 6:18).

As the glory – or light of God – reflected by the sun shone upon the Garden below, so light entered Noah's ark and the temple through a skylight or window(s) at the top edge(s) of Noah's ark (Gen. 6:16a, 8:6), and clerestory windows at the top edge(s) of the walls inside the Holy of Holies section of the temple (1 Kings 6:4). These windows in both the ark and the temple were designed for the purpose of ventilation and letting in light.

Many Masonic lodges throughout the world have named them-selves after Solomon and also after certain aspects of the temple. Some lodges go by the name "dormer" in reference to the window(s) on the top of the wall inside the temple's "holies" where it met with the roof. Scripture tells us that "The windows were covered" (Ezek. 41:16b). The coverings on the windows were most probably lattice, which immediately brings to my mind the verse, "Behold, he stands behind our wall; he is looking through the windows, gazing through the lattice" (Song of Sol. 2:9b).

As mentioned earlier, the outer walls of the temple, like the outer walls of the Garden of Eden, were made of stone, but its inner walls were of wood. It is tempting to suppose that Jachin and Boaz – the two great pillars at the doorway to the Temple – had some allusion to the two trees in the midst of the Garden of Eden (the tree of life and the tree of the knowledge of good and evil). For there was a bowl-shaped capital that sat atop each of the eighteen-cubit-high pil-lars and carved all around the outside of the capitals were hundreds of pomegranates. Was "the fruit" placed out of reach?

"He made a lattice network, with wreaths of chain work, for the capitals which were on top of the pillars: seven chains for one capital and seven for the other capital" (1 Kings 7:17). Did these chains, per-haps, symbolize the barring of the way to the fruit of the two trees? Perhaps there is also passing reference to the tree of life in Aaron's budding rod kept in the Ark of the Covenant in the Holy of Holies.

Access to the temple was gained by passing between these two great pillars bearing the representation of hundreds of pomegranates covered in chains. Was the forbidden fruit Adam ate a pomegranate perhaps? The Bible doesn't specifically say what kind of fruit Adam ate, but it's interesting to note that the word "pomegranate" derives from the Latin *pomum* ("apple") and *granatus* ("seeded"). The French refer to it as *le grenade*. Did Adam before the Fall know that he was holding, as it were, a "grenade" in his hand?

Regarding the threatened punishment for eating of the fruit of the tree of the knowledge of good and evil, the serpent said to Eve in the garden before the Fall, "'You will not surely die. For God knows that in the day you eat of it your eyes will be opened, and you will be like God, knowing good and evil.' So when the woman saw that the tree was good for food, that it was pleasant to the eyes, and a tree desirable to make one wise, she took of its fruit and ate. She also gave to her husband with her, and he ate'" (Gen. 3:4b–6). Thus Adam and Eve tried to obtain unlawfully what Solomon had requested and received lawfully. For, when the LORD God invited Solomon to request of Him anything, Solomon replied, "Therefore give to Your servant an understanding heart to judge Your people, that I may discern between good and evil" (1 Kings 3:9).

Adam and Eve thought that wisdom was simply to "know" good and evil. But Solomon asked God for wisdom to know the difference, i.e., to "discern between" good and evil. Thus, true wisdom is the ability to distinguish good from bad. Therefore, wisdom lies in the ability to discern. However, the LORD God, not man, is the arbiter of what is good and what is bad in every sphere of life. Solomon sought wisdom primarily to judge or govern his people.

Solomon's wisdom was soon put to the test upon the death of an infant of one of two harlots who had given birth at the same time. Both claimed the living infant as their own. Solomon asked for a sword that the child might be divided in order that each woman might receive half. One woman thought that a fair judgment. The other woman offered to give up her claim to the child so that it might live, and Solomon discerned that she was the true mother. "And all Israel heard of the judgment which the king had rendered; and they feared the king, for they saw that the wisdom of God was in him to administer justice" (1 Kings 3:28).

All feuds among people, including the feud between the two women in Solomon's day, began when Adam and Eve rebelled against God by eating the fruit thereby putting enmity between man and God and between man and creation.

King Solomon was building for 20 years, seven of which were spent building the Temple. The amount of stone quarried and the amount of trees felled for raw material was phenomenal. But the peace, harmony, and cooperation between the men and nations involved is even more marvelous to consider. Solomon and Solomon's kingdom was a type of Christ and Christ's kingdom.

Freddy

*W*EE JAMIE, our Sydney Silky terrier I introduced earlier, was creating a fuss in the grass behind the coop that housed the twenty-odd pigeons I kept when we lived at the manse in the North Pine suburb of the northwestern reaches of Brisbane. He was right next to the lady-finger banana trees, and I thought that Wee Jamie had found a dead parrot. When I reached down to pick it up, I noticed it wasn't dead when it latched on to the fleshy part of my hand between the thumb and forefinger of my right hand! Ah-ouch! I also noticed it was not a parrot, but a smaller rainbow lorikeet.

There was a tennis court next to the manse and the lorikeets that zigzagged in the air around the place with great rapidity would, on occasion, collide with the chain-link fence with all the wallop of a Roger Federer serve! Obviously this rainbow lorikeet had suffered some internal damage when he collided with the fence. It was close to evening, so I put the lorikeet, whom I decided to call Freddy, in a cardboard box for his safety. I fully expected him to be dead by morning. Come morning, I opened the box to find Freddy lying on his back in the same way he had been when I had found him the previous day. It then registered with me – for the second time – that he wasn't as dead as I had anticipated when he sunk his "teeth" into the same fleshy part of my hand as before!

It took weeks, but Freddy slowly began to recuperate with the aid of the tender loving care I kept supplying him. Rainbow lorikeets eat mainly nectar. What a beautiful looking bird! What a sweet singing-voice he had, too! Eventually I started tossing him in the air to help him learn to fly again. He would gently glide and land not far away on the grass in front of my pigeon hut. Surely he would make a full recovery!

Robert, my brother-in-law, had a large, enclosed pen at his place in Collingwood Park where he had been keeping his pet sulphur-crested cockatoo, which had recently flown away. It seemed like a good idea when he suggested that Freddy might appreciate the safety of the spacious bird pen to gain full recovery of flight. I agreed and we placed Freddy in his new pen. Robert never really told me what became of Freddy – only that, one day, Freddy was gone. But gone where?

Christ's Kingdom

ONE greater and wiser than Solomon is here. And the coming of the Messiah, or Christ, was prophesied throughout the Old Testament Scriptures. After the Fall of man in the Garden of Eden, the LORD God promised to send One who would crush the serpent's head, in other words, to destroy the devil and all his works. For when speaking to the serpent – who was used as an instrument by Satan in the Fall of man – the LORD God said,

> Because you have done this, you are cursed more than all cattle, and more than every beast of the field; on your belly you shall go, and you shall eat dust all the days of your life. And I will put enmity between you and the woman, and between your seed and her Seed; He shall bruise your head, and you shall bruise His heel. (Genesis 3:14–15)

The rest of the Bible makes it very clear that by speaking to the serpent, the LORD God is addressing Satan who has deluded the whole world and whose seed are those who remain deluded by him and through their own sins remain in spiritual bondage to him. Thus, the Seed of the woman, ultimately, is Jesus Christ together with all who are "in Him." Christ saved His people by having died in their stead and having been physically raised from the dead. At some point in their lives, the Holy Spirit regenerates, i.e., spiritually renews, those for whom He died. Thus, all who are born of His Spirit are His people and for them all the effects of the Fall will be totally removed by Jesus Christ – to a certain degree in this life, but completely when Jesus returns bodily.

Some view the Fall of man as a wrench of sorts in the works of God – something that somewhat thwarted the plan of God. To be sure, the Fall brought with it the horror of sin, misery, and death into the realm of humanity, and man now must toil hard to eat. But, paradoxically, the eating of the forbidden fruit was the means by which God "lubricated" the cogwheels of His creation-machine. For the Word becoming flesh was God in the Person of the Son entering into His creation to redeem mankind from God's justice. Thus, unlike Adam who placed creation into a state of decay, judgment, and death – Jesus, by His death and resurrection, places all that He redeems ultimately into a perfect condition of life everlasting.

Solomon asked God for wisdom. His request was ultimately fulfilled in Jesus Christ who is the wisdom of God incarnate. Thus, God ultimately replied to Solomon's request by giving him His only begotten Son, Jesus Christ. Christ and His kingdom is the anti-type of Solomon and his kingdom of peace. Christ brought His ever-expanding kingdom of peace with Him to earth. Christ's kingdom increases as Satan's kingdom is destroyed. The crucifixion and resurrection of Jesus was the destruction of Satan's kingdom in principle. The continual conversion and obedience to Christ of a multitude innumerable throughout the world throughout the centuries is the practical destruction of Satan's kingdom being realized.

Some 700 years before the actual event, Isaiah, under the inspiration of the Holy Spirit, spoke of the Lord Himself becoming flesh through His Son. Jesus Christ is "Immanuel," which translates to "God with us" (Is. 7:14; Matt 1:23). Isaiah also spoke of Christ bringing His kingdom of peace with Him,

> For unto us a Child is born, unto us a Son is given; and the government will be upon His shoulder. And His name will

be called Wonderful, Counselor, Mighty God, Everlasting
Father, Prince of Peace. Of the increase of His government
and peace there will be no end, upon the throne of David and
over His kingdom, to order it and establish it with judgment
and justice from that time forward, even forever. The zeal of
the LORD of hosts will perform this. (Isaiah 9:6–7)

The peace in Solomon's kingdom was merely a token of the ever-
increasing peace of the coming kingdom of Christ.

Isaiah also speaks of the universality of Christ's ever-increasing
kingdom of peace where he says,

Now it shall come to pass in the latter days that the mountain of the LORD's house shall be established on the top of
the mountains, and shall be exalted above the hills; and all
nations shall flow to it. Many people shall come and say,
'Come, and let us go up to the mountain of the LORD, to the
house of the God of Jacob; He will teach us His ways, and
we shall walk in His paths.' For out of Zion shall go forth
the law, and the word of the LORD from Jerusalem. He shall
judge between the nations, and rebuke many people; they
shall beat their swords into plowshares, and their spears
into pruning hooks; nation shall not lift up sword against
nation, neither shall they learn war anymore. (Isaiah 2:2–4)

The "house of the God of Jacob" and "Zion," as it turns out, are
the spiritual temple of God, i.e., wherever people anywhere on earth
gather in the name of Jesus Christ. The God who dwelt between the
cherubim in the Holy of Holies in the Temple at Jerusalem – now,
since the Day of Pentecost, dwells by His Spirit in His people across
the face of the whole earth. Which is to say that Christ's kingdom
spreads on earth with the spread of true Christianity – wherever
people become obedient to the true Gospel. Wherever people keep
doing "all things" to the glory of God, there is Christ's kingdom.
Christ's kingdom is spiritual, but that does not mean that it is not
solidly grounded in God's creation. For just as it did for the first
man (Adam), so it does for the second Man (Jesus, who is the last

Adam) – the Cultural Mandate still stands. The mandate for man to continually develop creation is being fulfilled even today. Christ, through and by His Holy Spirit, is working invisibly in the hearts of all human beings, many savingly.

Jesus went to great lengths to demonstrate that He had been raised from the dead with the same body He had when He was nailed to the cross. Thus, by being raised bodily from the dead, He is the beginning of God's new humanity – the "first fruits." He is the beginning of God's new creation. The resurrected Jesus is made of the same "material" as you and me. Thus, included in Christ's redemption of mankind is the renewal and transformation of this present creation.

1) Behold! The mountain of the Lord,
   In latter days shall rise
   On mountain tops above the hills,
   And draw the wond'ring eyes.

2) To this the joyful nations round,
   all tribes and tongues shall flow;
   up to the hill of God, they'll say,
   and to His house we'll go.

3) The beam that shines from Zion's hill
   shall lighten ev'ry land;
   The King who reigns in Salem's tow'rs
   Shall all the world command.

4) Among the nations He shall judge;
   His judgments truth shall guide;
   His sceptre shall protect the just,
   And quell the sinner's pride.

5) No strife shall rage, nor hostile feuds
   disturb those peaceful years;
   to ploughshares men shall beat their swords,
   to pruning hooks their spears.

6) No longer hosts encount'ring hosts
   shall crowds of slain deplore;
   they hang the trumpet in the hall,
   and study war no more.

7) Come then, O house of Jacob! come
    to worship at His shrine;
    And, walking in the light of God,
    with holy beauties shine.
    — Isaiah 2:2–6,
    Paraphrase 18, RCH

Wee Jamie

WEE JAMIE, our dog, never seemed to fully recover from the time he was ill in Brisbane. It was a Sunday morning and I was getting ready to lead the worship service at the North Pine Presbyterian Church. We lived in the manse, right next door to the church building. Jamie's back legs were going away from him, and he was very disoriented. It seemed that all the vets in Brisbane were strict Sabbatarians, for trying to get hold of a vet was as useless as trying to flag down a taxi on the Island of Lewis on the Sabbath!

There was one vet who answered her phone, but wouldn't hear of us bringing our sick animal to her. I told her Wee Jamie's symptoms. She replied with one word, "Teek." "Teek?" I said back to her. I asked if she could repeat the word. "Teek," is all she said. I asked if she could put the word in a sentence. She obliged by saying, "Your dog has a teek." Ah, a tick.

While I conducted the worship service, a member of the congregation drove Dorothy and Wee Jamie to an Emergency Veterinary Hospital somewhere across town. The viruses carried by these ticks can cause paralysis, even death in dogs.

When they arrived, Dot was immediately held to ransom. They had the antidote, but it might cost up to $1,000 to administer. "Should we go ahead?" Decisions! Decisions! It did end up costing us $400 and Wee Jamie had to stay overnight for observation. We were given the all clear to bring him home and we were happy to have our Sydney silky terrier back. But he was different. He seemed to be a lot more introverted, if a dog can be like that.

He was a good wee dog the first year we moved to the cooler climate of Tasmania. I would take him for bush walks. Then he started refusing to come with me. I'm sure the neighbours thought the wee dog was being murdered as I tried to coax him to keep walking every time he kept turning round and wanting to head back for home. No more walks for Wee Jamie. He just ate and slept.

On the fourth year into our stay in Tasmania, Wee Jamie was close to turning 16. He started having the odd "accident" on the kitchen floor and, worse, sometimes even on the carpet! We had taken him to the local vet and were told that he was about ready to "buy the farm." He had a heart problem (backwash), a bowel problem (incontinent), an eye problem (nearly blind), a hearing problem (deaf as a doorpost), and he was covered in warts that were starting to bleed. According to the vet, the warts were causing him a great deal of pain. That's why Wee Jamie didn't like affection! We were hurting him whenever we petted him. He retreated away from us and would only engage us when, like a grumpy old man, he would bark his commands at us to feed him!

We were to be at the vet's office on Friday at 4 o'clock. We had his favourite blanket with him, and a little furry kangaroo toy that he had had since we got him as a puppy. He was given a sedative to calm him down since Wee Jamie never liked going to the vet even at the best of times. About twenty minutes later, the vet administered a green liquid that would forever put him to sleep. Dorothy was howling as she stroked him. I stroked him, too, as I tried to fight back the tears of nearly sixteen years of affection for this pet. Sure, some farmers are able just to shoot their dogs without batting an eyelid when they're done with them, but Wee Jamie had been my good mate for years.

I had already dug a hole for Jamie in our backyard. The thought of his dead and limp body being thrown in the back of a garbage truck spurred me on to dig deeper. We took our wee dead pet dog home, wrapped him in his blanket, and buried him in our backyard with his toy kangaroo placed between his front paws. If the neighbours saw us, they would have thought we were burying a loved one! We planted a tree to mark his grave. It took about a month for us to get over it all.

True Peace and Harmony

ULTIMATELY, true Christianity is about lasting and true peace and harmony – peace and harmony with God and with His laws, between nations, with each other, and within us – all to the greater glory of God. The message of the Gospel of Peace is about the reconciliation with God that Jesus Christ has purchased for all who will believe in Him. Jesus fixed what Adam broke when Adam, as mankind's representative, ate of the tree of the knowledge of good and evil in Garden of Eden. As a Man, and for mankind, Jesus did what Adam failed to do: He kept every aspect of God's Law perfectly, and He paid the death-penalty man owed to God for breaking the first covenant arrangement in the Garden.

After being bodily resurrected and having bodily ascended into Heaven, the Mediator – the Man Christ Jesus – received from God that which God had promised Adam before the Fall should he have kept the covenant. Jesus kept that same covenant perfectly and received for His perfect obedience the afore-promised everlasting life rather than the conversely threatened death for disobedience. However, Jesus didn't receive only for Himself that which God had promised, He received it also for all who would receive Him – those for whom He shed His own blood. The shed blood of all the Old Testament sacrifices typified this great blessing: The redemption of the people of God and their world.

In the garden, God had conversely promised man everlasting life when He threatened death to Adam (and through him, all men) should he break God's Law that God has written on every man's heart. The everlasting life promised was essentially an everlasting – and therefore unbreakable – loving relationship or communion between God and man. However, this didn't simply mean that Adam and Eve and their future offspring would get to mill around the Garden of Eden forevermore, as it was when they were first created. Rather it means that Heaven would become united forever and all time with Earth. In other words, had Adam not broken his probation in the Garden but had instead successfully completed it, the new heavens and the new earth could have been brought in then.

The obedient "Adam" (Jesus Christ) is progressively bringing the new heavens and the new earth into being as His kingdom spreads. Like a mustard seed growing into a tree, His kingdom is expanding, and like leaven in a batch of dough, the influence of His kingdom is increasing throughout all of creation and into creation's every sphere. On the Last Day all will be revealed, and all will be renewed.

1) Lo! What glorious sight appears
   to our admiring eyes!
   The former seas have pass'd away
   the former earth and skies.

2) From heav'n the New Jerus'lem comes,
   all worthy of its Lord;
   See all things now at last renew'd,
   And paradise restor'd!

— Rev. 21:1–2,
Paraphrase 67, RCH

Reflection

As I look back over my life, I can see where the invisible hand of God was leading me. He was leading the wanderer – the "prodigal son" – back to the Father's house. He was leading me out of the wilderness and into the Promised Land. He was leading me to

Eden, but not the same Eden in which Adam lived, rather the new Eden that the Man Christ Jesus lives in with all His redeemed. The old Eden has been developed and renewed! However, it is no less a real physical place than the former Eden. Just as the cedars of Lebanon were sawn into planks in Solomon's sawmill for the building of his kingdom to the glory of God, so the "trees" of Christ's Eden, in a manner of speaking, are presently being used in the building of His kingdom to the glory of God, as Christ, by His Spirit, works in the hearts of men and women in their every sphere of activity. Therefore, since this earth belongs to Jesus Christ, even non-Christians are presently working for Him and will forfeit their earthly labour to Him. On the Last Day, Christ will purge creation of sin and the residue of sin, leaving that which is pleasing to Him. The devil therefore will have no victory! "For this purpose the Son of God was manifested, that He might destroy the works of the devil" (1 John 3:8b). And notice that the works of those who consciously labour for Christ and His kingdom are not lost, for they will "rest from their labours, and their works follow them" (Rev. 14:13b). Job looked forward to standing on his own two (resurrected) feet, on solid ground, and seeing his Redeemer also standing on earth (Job 19:25–27).

On account of the influence of pagan philosophy, many people today tend to adopt a materialistic life and worldview, which is to say that even though some people might acknowledge the spiritual nature of things, we have a tendency to view reality and the things we do in the world on a purely physical level. In fact, the prevailing philosophy in the West separates the physical from the spiritual. But just because spiritual things are spiritually discerned doesn't mean that the spiritual is not inherent in the physical, that is, in nature. Nature *is* spiritual.

All creation reflects the Creator, who is Spirit, and man, who is spiritual and the very image of God. Therefore, God's reflection is seen in the physical realm – including us. We noted this earlier when we talked about the one and the many aspect seen in creation. We know God from the things He has made, but, because of our sin, we will not look upon Him. And because of our sin, neither will He look upon us, unless we are first reconciled to Him through Christ's provision for our sin. Christ's cross is the place of reconciliation, for that is where God's love covers a multitude of sins. Christ's shed blood cleanses of all iniquity those to whom it is spiritually applied by the Holy Spirit. This spiritual cleansing – i.e., the Spirit and the sanctifying blood of Christ being sprinkled or poured on believers and their children – is depicted in Covenant Baptism (referenced earlier). It is also depicted in God's shedding the blood of innocent animals in order to provide a suitable "covering," i.e., animal skins, for the sin problem introduced by Adam and Eve.

Robert M. Pirsig, in his book with the captivating title *Zen and the Art of Motorcycle Maintenance*, illustrates what I mean by "knowing" God but not seeing Him. Pirsig wrestles with the universal problem of the one and the many. He refers to the "one" aspect of reality as "classic" and the "many" aspect as "romantic." He says these two ways of viewing reality have been inherited by the West from the ancient Greek philosophers. He attempts to reconcile or marry the two by using the idea of "quality."

The long and the short of it is that though Pirsig, in the course of his philosophical musings over the one and the many even mentions the Trinity, fails to see the God he speaks of! I believe this is a clear case of not being able to see the forest for the trees. Pirsig is speaking of "quality" when he ought to be speaking of the Triune God, who alone is the determiner of what is good and what is evil. From what I can see, Pirsig has substituted the abstract "quality" for the true and living God.

Only God is good; therefore, only God is the true measure of quality. Only the Triune God is the measure of good and evil, right and wrong. Solomon asked for the gift that would enable him to be a good ruler, i.e., "wisdom," which, we discover through Scripture, is "to test everything against God." Thus, the "one" has quality and the "many" has quality, not because I say so, but because God says so. Therefore, God is the absolute concerning "quality control."

I enjoyed Pirsig's book. It is a book on philosophy. But, I believe, in his book, philosophy is Pirsig's undoing because he views everything he can see of reality in philosophical terms. Thus, he discerns the character of the true and living God – the blessed Trinity as seen in the "one" and the "many" aspects of creation – to be some philosophical equation. He's so close to the kingdom – and yet so far!

The problem of the one and the many, inherent in all creation, can be reconciled only by observing the equal ultimacy of the Godhead, because all creation reflects its Creator – including mankind.

I was reminded of this the night when I, with my wife and our three daughters, became Australian citizens. At the ceremony, together with six hundred new Australian citizens, we sang a song, which, along with "Waltzing Matilda," is another unofficial Australian Anthem. Here are the words of the chorus of the song we sang:

> We are one, but we are many
> And from all the lands on earth we come.
> We share a dream and sing with one voice:
> I am, you are, we are Australian.
> I am, you are, we are Australian.
>
> – Bruce Woodley and Dobe Newton

Nina and "Popeye"

WHILE we were staying at Lorna Street in Brown Plains, I had a big fish tank with an assortment of subtropical fish in it including angelfish, swordtails, platys, guppies, and the like. I also had a black "goldfish" that we called Popeye. He was one of those blimpy-goldfish with a Victorian long, black skirt-tail and bulging eyeballs. Popeye was comical to see. One of my twin daughters, Nina, who was about 8 years old or so at the time, really loved Popeye, who would come to the glass when anyone approached – especially Nina.

One day Nina was terribly upset. Popeye was floating upside down on the surface. (That's a bad sign when your goldfish is "swimming" upside down!) He was really grey looking. Nina asked if I would pray for Popeye. I must admit (with all the major problems in the world) I felt a wee bit silly praying that God would heal a sick fish! But I knew that God was interested in the small and seemingly insignificant things in our lives. And I knew that He cared about the feelings of His little children. Further, I knew that innocent faith expressed by his children is pleasing to Him, so I prayed something like this: "Heavenly Father, Nina is really upset about Popeye's condition. Would You be pleased to make Popeye well again? In Jesus' name. Amen." Nina thanked me for praying as she reached her little hand into the water and set Popeye right way up. And, what do you know? The colour began to return into Popeye and he made a full recovery!

Popeye lived for a long while after this, but we came home one day to find him dried out and stuck to the living room carpet. Another bad sign! He was a goner this time. But there would be none of the "flush him down the toilet" treatment for Popeye! Nina had me bury her wee friend in the backyard. Her two sisters laughed at the idea of attending Popeye's "funeral," but Nina and I stood in the rain while we buried her beloved Popeye. A stone with "Popeye" written on it was placed to mark the grave.

Reconciliation

As Christ's kingdom spreads, more and more nations shall beat their swords into ploughshares and their spears into pruning hooks till eventually there will be worldwide peace. Why? Because reconciliation between man and God has been brought about by the life, death, resurrection, ascension, and session* of Jesus Christ. His kingdom grows by the poured out Holy Spirit working with the proclamation of His Word.

---

* Session: Christ being *seated* "at the right hand of God as our sovereign high priest, pleading the virtue of His once-for-all atoning sacrifice on behalf of His people" (see Psa. 110:1; Acts 2:34, 35; Heb. 1:3; 9:24; 10:12; 1 Pet. 3:22). Alan Cairns, *Dictionary of Theological Terms*, Expanded Edition. Greenville, SC: Ambassador Emerald International, 2002, 415.

I believe in a future Golden Age before the Lord's return – an age of peace and harmony among the nations. The motto of the City of Glasgow, Scotland, captures something of the spirit of this where it says, "Let Glasgow flourish by the preaching of Thy Word." Thus, the Spirit will work with the Word in individual hearts in the midst of people to the point where even whole cities (e.g., Geneva under Calvin) and even entire nations (e.g., Scotland under Knox) submit themselves to the rulership of Jesus Christ and "flourish"! This is not to say that everyone on the planet earth will be converted to Christianity before Jesus Christ's bodily return. But it is to say that the earth will eventually be fully Christianized. "For the earth will be filled with the knowledge of the glory of the LORD, as the waters cover the sea" (Hab. 2:14). Solomon and the spread of his kingdom were a type of Christ and the spread of His kingdom.

For when the Christian is focused on the glory of God in all things, even the universal problem of the one and the many is reconciled. The "one" ceases to war against the "many" and vice versa. For all things are reconciled by and in Jesus Christ who is the express image of God – the original One and Many. Jesus is the only Mediator between God and men. Additionally, Jesus is God and Man in one divine Person forever, so Jesus is the picture of God and man in perfect peace and harmony forever. Perfect peace and harmony in any and every sphere thus begins with Jesus. Therefore, there will be true and lasting peace and harmony among nations only when they, by His Spirit working with His Word, submit to the authority of Jesus Christ.

Has there been and are there any Christian, i.e., Christianized, nations today? Many European nations at the time of the Protestant Reformation submitted to Christ's rulership. Indeed, are not the Western nations "Christian" nations? What makes a nation Christian? A Christian nation is that which acknowledges Christ and the Triune God and has based its laws on His Ten Commandments. Therefore, we have seen "tokens" of Christ's kingdom of peace and harmony in nations even in fairly recent times.

This doesn't mean that everyone in the nation is a Christian, as my Scottish upbringing attests! I was taught two competing life and worldviews while attending public school. That's madness! For one life and worldview is Christ-centered and the other is anti-Christian. Evolution and Christianity cannot be reconciled because they are mutually exclusive. Either God created creation, including us – as He has revealed in His written Word – or the world and everything in it is the product of random chance (as postulated by fallen men, i.e., Darwinists), which means we are utterly lacking in accountability to one another since we are not accountable to a god, and there is no moral standard, i.e., God's Ten Commandments, which instructs us on how we are to relate to God and our fellow man.

The evolutionist must first be regenerated by God in His grace before he will submit his thoughts to God speaking through Christ in His written Word. Otherwise he will remain in his rebellion against God and His revelation (whether written or things created). By holding to his anti-Christian theory, the evolutionist demonstrates that he has no real peace with God. But God is gracious. He permits the evolutionist to war against Him – till God draws the last breath from him or converts him! I was at war with God till He took my breath from me, so to speak. Only then (by God's grace alone) did I surrender to Jesus Christ who says, "I am the way, the truth, and the life. No one comes to the Father except through Me" (John 14:6).

Thanks to God I now no longer have the brain imbalance I had in my youth from my faulty Scottish education. Only by the grace of God in Jesus Christ am I now fully clothed (in Christ's righteousness) and in my right mind. For if the theory of evolution is true, then God is a liar, which would mean that the Triune God didn't create Adam as He says He did in His Word. And if God didn't create Adam, then Adam never sinned. And if Adam never sinned, then Jesus never died for sinners. And if Jesus never died for sinners, then He has not reconciled us to God. And if we have not been reconciled to God, then we are still at war with God and utterly lost. And if there is no God, then there is no Law of God, which also means that there is no Day of Judgment. This in turn means that we all might as well behave like the animals the evolutionist insists we've come from! But this, in the final analysis, is simply to kick against the goads. For God is!

The evolutionist needs a new pair of glasses through which to view his world. Like the rest of mankind, the evolutionist needs to see reality through God's Word in order to get a proper and undistorted view of the world. Otherwise, in his blindness, he forfeits everything – including his own soul! As John Calvin explains:

> God has appointed to His children alone the whole world and all that is in it. For this reason, they are also called the heirs of the world; for at the beginning Adam was appointed to be lord of all, on this condition, that he should continue in obedience to God. Accordingly, his rebellion against God deprived him of the right, which had been bestowed on him, not only himself, but his posterity. And since all things are subject to Christ, we are fully restored by His mediation – and that through faith. Therefore, all that unbelievers enjoy may be regarded as the property of others, which they rob or steal. And which of us would venture to claim as his own a single grain of wheat if he were not taught by the Word of God that he is the heir of the world? Common sense, indeed, pronounces that the wealth of the world is naturally intended for our use; but, since dominion over the world was taken from us in Adam, everything that we touch of the gifts of God becomes defiled by our pollution. So then, all things become unclean to us until God graciously comes to our aid. By ingrafting us into his Son, He constitutes us anew to be lords of the world, that we may lawfully use as our own all the wealth with which He supplies us. Justly, therefore, does Paul connect lawful enjoyment with "the Word," by which alone we regain that which was lost in Adam; for we must acknowledge God as our Father, that we may be His heirs, and Christ as our Head, that those things which are His may become ours.*

---

* John Calvin, *Commentaries* – Ephesians to Jude; on 1 Tim. 4:3–5. Associated Publishers and Authors, Wilmington, Delaware, 2193–2194.

Fionna and the Chipmunks

IONNA was 2 going on 3 when a Masonic lodge friend invited us to join his wife and mother-in-law at his cottage at a lake in Manitoba. Close to the lake there was a big creek that ran over rocks rubbed smooth by the advancing and retreating glaciers of long ago. There were colourful frogs aplenty, fish by the shoal, and lots of little hummingbirds hovering around the blooming, vibrantly-colored flowers. Some of the cottagers had filled their hummingbird feeders with nectar. It was great fun to watch those colourful and amazing little creatures do their unique thing!

Another highlight was the feeding of the chipmunks. Chipmunks are the cutest of all the furry little woodland critters – and they were eating right out of our hands! We called Fionna to come and see the wee chipmunks. We told her, "They're really cute. You'll love them." But Fionna was hiding in the cottage. When asked what was wrong, she replied with a phrase that's been repeated in our family ever since: In a frightened little voice she said, "No like monkeys!"

It was only after a great deal of persuasion and explanation of the difference between monkeys and chip*munks* that Fionna finally delighted herself along with the rest of us in feeding the creatures!

Christ Moments

OD alone brings about the true conversion of any individual. The individual is transformed from being part of the old humanity that, in Adam, is dead in its trespasses and sins. God brings about that conversion first by regenerating the individual, i.e., enabling him to believe in the story and the message of the Gospel. The Gospel is the good news about the reconciliation God has brought about through Jesus Christ. It is particularly good news to those who believe it. For the regenerated Christian, reconciliation with God brings with it, among many other things, a new appreciation of the things of God.

One of the things I began to appreciate is the order God has put in His creation, which I first began to notice while viewing the starry night sky. I wanted to know who put the stars there. Thus began my quest for knowledge and understanding – not of the stars – but rather of the One who made them and placed them in their unique formations. In hindsight, I was encountering God every time I thought about the nature of the Being who could create the heavens and the earth and all that is in them.

Adam was encountering God when he named all the animals in the Garden, and when he saw Eve for the first time, for he understood the very essence or nature of each creature just by observing it. By his observations, he was seeing revelation of the Creator. Solomon, on account of the Fall, encountered God in a more limited way than the pre-Fall Adam when he studied and named the flora and fauna. But, still, Solomon encountered the living and true God by seeing His reflection in these created things.

Though we are able to make categorical distinctions, everything in creation is related. There are many fields or spheres of study. Yet God can be encountered in every sphere. Take gravity, for example. By throwing a stone in the air and watching it fall back down, we may observe gravitational forces or laws. The stone behaves the way it does because that's how God designed the laws of gravity to work. When anything "works" in any particular sphere of activity, it works because it is operating in accordance with God's laws in that particular sphere. There are "built in" laws in every sphere.

A nation, which is "one" (e.g., Scotland, Canada, Australia), may have "many" spheres of human activity and endeavour. Three basic spheres are family, church, and state. These three basic spheres of human activity are distinct, yet each interpenetrates the others. There are laws that belong only to particular spheres of the nation, yet these laws serve to compliment the "oneness" of the nation. It's not hard to see God's reflection in this when we consider the distinctions between the Father and the Son and the Holy Spirit who interpenetrate each other in the Godhead. Therefore, to consider any sphere of human activity on its own is akin to considering each Person of the Godhead on His own.

An already alluded-to book that got me thinking about encountering God through the things He has made was, strangely enough, Robert M. Pirsig's *Zen and the Art of Motorcycle Maintenance*. Pirsig mentions in an author's note that what he says in his book "…should in no way be associated with that great body of factual information relating to orthodox Zen Buddhist practice. It's not very factual on motorcycles either."[!]

Though Pirsig in his book teaches nothing about Zen Buddhist practice, I began to wonder what the Zen Buddhist is trying to attain. It appears to me – if I have understood the practice of Zen Buddhism correctly – that he is seeking something more than just a happy equilibrium in the centre of his being, i.e., peace and harmony with himself and within himself through meditation. Instead, he is actually seeking "enlightenment," which literally means "to understand." I can relate to that!

The Zen Buddhist is seeking a deep and lasting enlightenment or understanding, which, he believes, consists in and of a true understanding of nature. He believes that a true understanding of nature can be found wrapped up in life's daily activities. It is during the process of "unwrapping" that the Zen Buddhist supposedly catches glimpses of the lasting enlightenment he seeks.

Both Zen and Masonry fall short of glorifying God through Jesus Christ. I believe some of these glimpses, or, if you will, "Zen moments," are likely God-encounters. But since these "encounters" are purely of the subjective sort, they serve only the person experiencing the encounter. These encounters perhaps are mere glimpses of God through the lattice – that most likely will not cause the recipient to fall on his face and worship the God to whom we must all give account. However, I don't believe that God-encounters are limited only to Zen Buddhists, but are to be found in every activity that engages the mind. Adam and Solomon named animals and plants. All creation speaks of God.

The Christian, of course, would insist that true understanding and true lasting peace and harmony in any and every sphere can only come through Jesus Christ. "Zen moments" are merely signposts. They are more properly "Christ moments." They are not the end of the road (or destination), they are only the beginning of the way; for Christ says, "I am the way, the truth and the life. No one comes to the Father except through Me" (John 14:6).

Thinking back to when I was young, I wanted to run like a deer. But I noticed that when I started to run, I would often get a sharp pain in my side. However, if I pressed on and didn't stop, there would come a moment when the stitch left me and it seemed I could run almost effortlessly. Likewise when I was rowing, there would come a moment when all four of us were in perfect sync – our oars, dipping in and out of the water without splashing, propelling the boat forward with the greatest of ease. I found myself longing for those moments when, with mind, body, and soul in sync, I obeyed the laws of physics. There is that rare moment when the laws work with you and for you instead of against you, as was my usual experience. The experience is sublime, spiritual – it is a "letting the saw do the work" moment! But, again, such experiences are only signposts pointing to Christ and His kingdom. Thus, I call them "Christ moments."

As we contemplate these things, one is reminded of a few verses from Isaiah: "Have you not known? Have you not heard? The everlasting God, the LORD, the Creator of the ends of the earth, neither faints nor is weary. His understanding is unsearchable. He gives power to the weak, and to those who have no might He increases strength. Even the youths shall faint and be weary, and the young men shall utterly fall, but those who wait on the LORD shall renew their strength; they shall mount up with wings like eagles, they shall run and not be weary, they shall walk and not faint" (Is. 40:28–31).

Because there are laws at work in every sphere of our daily activities, we may experience Christ moments in every sphere. These moments are also flashes of light affording the soul glimpses of perfect peace and harmony, between ourselves and our surroundings and between ourselves and our Creator, small cameos that give us a sort of foretaste of Christ's kingdom. A musician will occasionally experience them when composing a tune or song – usually when he hits that "special" chord progression or note sequence – likewise the poet, when he gets the meter and word rhythm to coincide with the mood he's trying to portray and convey. The mathematician will notice them, too. These are discoveries every bit as exhilarating as those experienced by the old explorers finding new lands or territories. Even the modern social experiment called "multiculturalism," of which I spoke earlier, as it wrestles with the issues of the one and the many, and unity and diversity, will almost seem to have its Christ moments.

Surely these Christ moments are real reflections of the peace and harmony of the Triune God. For are they not mirrored experiences of the equal ultimacy of the "One" and the "Many" – perfect peace and harmony? And since no one can come to the Father except through Jesus Christ, Christ is the tangent point of *all* our experiences of God. Therefore, Christ needs to be the Head of every sphere of our lives in order for that sphere to work for us to the glory of God and not against us.

> 1) O for a closer walk with God,
>   A calm and heavenly frame,
>   A light to shine upon the road
>   That leads me to the Lamb!
>
> 6) So shall my walk be close with God,
>   Calm and serene my frame;
>   So purer light shall mark the road
>   That leads me to the Lamb.
>
> — William Cowper (1731–1800)
> Hymn 457, RCH

New Life and Worldview

*I*T's great being able to see God's fingerprints and footprints all over His creation. How could I have been so blind for so long? And how could I have considered the theory of evolution to be even remotely true? I'm glad my childhood "brain imbalance" is gone now that God has given me new life. Before He converted me, I read the Bible only from my own point of view. Now I read it from God's point of view! The worm on the ground with his worm's-eye view is now soaring as an eagle in the heavens with an eagle's-eye view of creation!

From the vantage point of God's Word, I can now see the Trinity as revealed in time – the past, the present, and the future! I can see what happened in the beginning. I can see something of what God is doing in the world today. And I can see the glorious future He has in store for those who, because of His condescending grace, love Him.

God created the heavens and the earth at the very beginning. He has redeemed it and is progressively renewing it. And in the end, He will have completely renewed the heavens and the earth.

Creation's renewal began with the bodily resurrection of Jesus Christ from the dead. He is the Son of God, but also the Son of Man, including being made of the dust of this creation. Thus, the dust of creation was sanctified the moment Jesus entered into Heaven upon His bodily ascension. He is coming back with the same body He had when He died on the cross and was raised again.

Jesus said, "Destroy this temple, and in three days I will raise it up" (John 2:19). Those who heard Him say this thought He was talking about the Temple in Jerusalem, but "He was speaking of the temple of His body" (John 2:21). If Masonry had focused as much attention on Jesus Christ as it did Solomon's Temple, surely it would have helped me and countless others avoid a lot of the pitfalls, cesspools, swamps, and minefields superintended by the evil one! I am thankful that One greater than Solomon is here. I am thankful for His resurrection and His ascension into Heaven.

When He returns, all the graves and the sea will give up their dead, which is to say that our dead and decayed bodies will be regenerated, i.e., brought back to life in imperishable form. God made us in the beginning – He is able to remake us in the end. Those who belong to Jesus will face a future of eternal bliss because of God's grace. Those who have rejected Him will suffer eternally in the fires of Hell because of their sins. Jesus has satisfied God's justice for all those redeemed by Him.

I believe I'll see my mum and dad, my wife, and my grown children on the new earth, along with everyone who has been saved by the grace of God. All will have been raised physically from the dead. I believe that there will be fish, birds, and land animals (including monkeys and chipmunks!) on the new earth, though perhaps we will not find Diamond the dog, or Jock the jackdaw, Squawk the crow, Jamie the Sydney Silky, Popeye the goldfish, or Freddie the rainbow lorikeet. Though they all brought me joy, it is possible that these "old friends" may be gone forever. Heaven is everlasting life for man on the new earth with Jesus Christ. It is not about floating on clouds with a harp and a halo! The future is solid. It is concrete. It is real. It is not a theory or a philosophical equation. It is every bit as real as the resurrected and glorified Jesus Christ.

> Now I saw a new heaven and a new earth, for the first heaven and the first earth had passed away. And there was no more sea. Then I, John, saw the holy city, New Jerusalem, coming down out of heaven from God, prepared as a bride adorned for her husband. And I heard a loud voice from heaven saying, "Behold, the tabernacle of God is with men, and He will dwell with them, and they shall be His people. God Himself will be with them and be their God. And God will wipe away every tear from their eyes; there will be no more death, nor sorrow, nor crying. There will be no more pain, for the former things have passed away." (Rev. 21:1–4)

My old professor, Dr. Francis Nigel Lee, makes some insightful and helpful comments on these verses:

> The intimation that there will be no more Sea certainly seems to indicate that there will then indeed be Land and

Air and even River-water on the New Earth. Consequently, it will not be a brand-new and essentially different Earth, but rather our same Earth – re-new-ed and per-fect-ed. The material resurrection bodies within which we shall then live on that equally material and renewed Earth will be re-new-ed (yet not be brand new). They will not be essentially different bodies from those we now possess – but the same bodies as it were "re-tread-ed." They shall, says the Westminster Confession of Faith (32:2), be "these selfsame bodies and none other." On the other hand, though the New Earth to come after the Final Judgment will be essentially the same as this present Earth – it will indeed have a rather different appearance. Negatively, the New Earth will be without our Sea – and without man's sin or any of its consequences. And positively, the New Earth will then be this present Earth – developed to perfection. For at that time "there shall be no more death, neither sorrow, nor crying. Neither shall there be any more pain. For the former things [shall] have passed away." ... O Christian – let us then long for the advent of "that city which has foundations, whose Builder and Maker is God!" Meantime, let us thank Him for the wonderful foretaste of that city which we enjoy here and now in the Christian Church and in our Christian work in all fields of endeavour! Let us eat and drink and do all things here and now to the glory of God, knowing that our labours for the Lord are not in vain – and that our works follow us into glory! Let us firmly trust that we will indeed yet inherit the renewed Earth – and all its fullness! Too, let us even now bring all the natural resources of the Universe as well as all the cultural honour and glory of every Nation – into God's Kingdom. Thus shall we then... be able to enjoy it all not only today – but also both tomorrow on this present Earth, and forever in the hereafter too! So on then, Christian soldiers! Onward to victory! (Dr. Francis Nigel Lee, *John's Revelation Unveiled*, Ligstryders, 1999, 292–3; 303–4)

The Chief End

*I*T'S little wonder that we encounter God in Christ everywhere we turn, for the Apostle Paul, under inspiration of the Holy Spirit, says of Him,

> He is the image of the invisible God, the firstborn over all creation. For by Him all things were created that are in heaven and that are on earth, visible and invisible, whether thrones or dominions or principalities or powers. All things were created through Him and for Him. And He is before all things, and in Him all things consist. (Colossians 1:15–17)

J. M. Spier offers this fitting response, "[Man's] heart is the transcendent concentration point of all temporal functions, and from it he can direct his glance toward Him, through whom and unto whom are all things" (*An Introduction to Christian Philosophy*, Craig Press, 1954, 65).

I am thankful to God that He was and continues to be gracious toward me all the years of my life wherever I go on His great planet earth. I thank God for condescending to reveal Himself to me in His only begotten Son, and that He is patient with me. May He continue to be glorified as I enjoy Him daily now and forever. I thank Him that He was with me every inch of the way from Mason to Minister!

> Behold, he stands behind our wall;
> He is looking through the windows,
> Gazing through the lattice.

The End

Glossary

Ars Quatuor Coronatorum – Organized body of Masons who engage in Masonic research.

Blackballed – To have one's application to become a Freemason rejected by a local lodge.

Blue Lodge – Nickname for the body that confers the first three degrees of Freemasonry on account of the blue trappings that adorn their regalia.

Entered Apprentice – First degree of Freemasonry; one upon whom the First degree has been conferred.

Fellow Craft – Second degree of Freemasonry; one upon whom the Second degree has been conferred.

Freemason – Member of the Ancient Free and Accepted Masons.

Grand Lodge – Body of Masons overseeing local lodges in its jurisdiction.

Leviathan – Sea monster mentioned in Job 41:1f; see also Psalm 74:13 and 14. *Leviathan* is also the title of a 1651 book on political philosophy by Thomas Hobbes (1588–1679).

Lodge at work – Masons conferring degrees by performing rituals in the local lodge.

Mason – Member of the Ancient Free and Accepted Masons.

Masonic Lodge – Building where Freemasons meet to perform rituals.

Masonry – "What is Masonry? The erection of buildings and con-
secrating them to the veneration of God, we will admit was the
purpose of the builders, of the ancient operative art. The Masons
of the Speculative Science operate in a spiritual sense, employing
the tools of the operative Mason as symbols, and using veiled
allegories from the Bible to convey to their initiates a lesson and
belief that there is life beyond the grave (see 1 Kings 6:2; 1 Cor.
3:10–14)." (*The Bible and King Solomon's Temple in Masonry*, by
John Wesley Kelchner)

Master Mason – Third degree of Freemasonry; one upon whom the
first three degrees of Masonry have been conferred.

NWT, New World Translation – Version of the Bible used by Jehovah's
Witnesses.

Presbyterian – Name derived from the New Testament Greek word
presbuteros, meaning presbyter or elder. Emphasizing the form
of church government.

RCH, Revised Church Hymnary – Church of Scotland hymnbook
revised in 1929, containing Hymns, with the Scottish Psalter and
Scripture Paraphrases.

Red Lodge – Red Lodge comprised of bodies distinct but not separate
from Blue Lodge that cater to Master Masons seeking further
involvement in Freemasonry. So named for the red trapping adorn-
ing their regalia.

Reformed – Name given to the body of Christians who hold to the
Biblical doctrines taught by the Reformer John Calvin.

VOSL, or VSL – Volume of the Sacred Law. The Bible, and sometimes
other books, that sit, open, on the altar of a Masonic lodge at work.

Yabby – The Australian Aborigine name for a freshwater crayfish.

Confession of Faith[*]

1 I believe in God the Father Almighty, Maker of heaven and earth;
   And in Jesus Christ His only Son our Lord, Who was conceived of
   the Holy Ghost, Born of the Virgin Mary, Suffered under Pontius Pilate,
   Was crucified, dead, and buried; He descended into hell; The third day
   He arose again from the dead; He ascended into heaven, And sitteth
   on the right hand of God the Father Almighty; From thence He shall
   come to judge the quick and the dead. I believe in the Holy Ghost,
   the holy catholic Church, the communion of saints, the forgiveness of
   sins, the resurrection of the body, and life everlasting. Amen.[**]

2 I believe in one God, the Father Almighty, Maker of heaven and earth,
   and of all things visible and invisible: And in one Lord Jesus Christ,
   the only-begotten Son of God, begotten of His Father before all worlds;
   God of God, Light of Light, very God of very God; Begotten, not made,
   being of one substance with the Father, By whom all things were made:
   Who for us men, and for our salvation, came down from heaven, And
   was incarnate by the Holy Ghost of the Virgin Mary, And was made
   man, And was crucified also for us under Pontius Pilate. He suffered
   and was buried, And the third day He rose again according to the
   Scriptures, And ascended into heaven, And sitteth on the right hand
   of the Father; And He shall come again with glory to judge both the
   quick and the dead: Whose kingdom shall have no end. And I believe
   in the Holy Ghost, The Lord and Giver of Life, Who proceedeth from
   the Father and the Son, Who with the Father and the Son together is

---

[*] The historic creeds represent Christians' attempt to articulate sound doctrine. Jesus said the Word is the Seed (Matt. 13:19; Luke 8:11). This means the word is raw material, intended by God for man to plant and husband by faith, "till we all come to the unity of the faith and the knowledge of the Son of God, to a perfect man, to the measure of the stature of the fullness of Christ" (Eph. 4:13). During the early years, the church fought off many humanistic attempts to reduce the Word of God to things intellectually or psychologically palatable to man's sinful nature. The church made many such statements as the Apostles' Creed and the Nicene Creed in order to formulate mature expressions of the Seed. Time has proven that these affirmations very well represent the Biblical intent and establish the universals upon which a sound faith rest.

[**] The Apostles' Creed. While not written by the apostles themselves, the Apostles' Creed represents a summary of the apostles' teaching as found in Scripture and commonly circulated in the first hundred years of Christian history (Rousas John Rushdoony, *The Foundations of Social Order*. Vallecito, California: Ross House Books, 1998, 4).

worshipped and glorified, Who spake by the Prophets. And I believe
[in] one Holy Catholic and Apostolic Church. I acknowledge one Baptism for the remission of sins. And I look for the Resurrection of the
dead, And the life of the world to come. Amen.*

---

* THE NICENE CREED (Council of Nicæa, A.D. 325) elaborated the Apostles' Creed. It resolved a
theological question thrust upon the church by the Gnostics. The Gnostics believed in the typical Greek antithesis between the good *spirit, mind, or form* and the evil *material creation*.
This question revolved around whether Christ was of *one essence* with God (*homoousion*)
or merely of *like essence* with God (*homoiousion*). The Nicene Creed declares Christ to be
of "one substance" with the Father (Ibid., Rushdoony, 9–13).
    The historic church has embraced these creeds ever since, as attested by their frequent recital
in contemporary church services.

PHOTO BY BRENT NIMS

The Publisher's Word

All things are lawful for me, but all things are not helpful;
all things are lawful for me, but all things do not edify.

(1 Corinthians 10:23, NKJV)

NEIL MCKINLAY is quite an unusual fellow. First, his whole life appears as a poem, almost a Wordsworthian pastoral ode. He obviously loves God's creation and he obviously loves life. It makes sense then, that Neil McKinlay would travel the globe in search of his God and Savior.

How he found His Savior and Lord in pilgrimage is the story we now present. The poet unfolds his story with the relish and vigor of his youth. He captures our attention as he wanders like a cloud, because he strikes a responsive chord in our hearts. We would all love to be as sensitive and as sensible. Neil tells a man's story. He has worked hard, in earnest. The word *earnest* itself might comprehend the whole of Pastor McKinlay's story, were he not so inclined also to stop, smell the roses and simply enjoy the sky, the birds, the rural landscape – and their Creator. Moreover, he will entertain you with his travelogue and guided tour of places and things exotic for many of us. Yet he will also bear his soul in treating things that have tried it.

Lest we mislead the reader, this is also and fundamentally a story of how this seeker of life's meaning found a down payment in the fellowship of Freemasonry and its institutional deference to God. Most opposing treatments of Masonry merely attack and condemn the institution. Ordinarily, this approach does not win those who need the most to hear the truth. Rather, here you receive a measured, grateful, and even loving treatment of the institution, which necessarily concludes that there is yet a more excellent way (1 Corinthians 12:31).

Those who wish to read an accurate portrayal of Freemasonry will be pleased. Those who may be primarily familiar with Scottish Rite Masonry should find explanations of the differences between it and the York Rite lodge intriguing and sensible. For us Yanks, we know that many of America's honored founding fathers were lodge members, yet as Christians we harbor nagging reservations about this association. For men, so easily prone to error and in need of godly correction, it is refreshing to find a reasonable explanation for how apparently godly men might have associated themselves with an organization now so widely associated with the occult.

To expand this thought a bit further, we would share one intriguing example in *The Writings of George Washington*. Mr. Snyder, a clergyman, wrote Washington to alert him of increasing subversion of American Masonic lodges with the doctrines of the Illuminati. Washington responded in writing on September 25, 1798 from Mount Vernon. Washington could not comment on the book to which Rev. Snyder alluded, but confirmed the "nefarious and dangerous plan and doctrines of the Illuminati."* (This influence in America arose out of some misguided sympathy with the French Revolution, and so a number of men embraced its philosophies and policies of the Enlightenment and French Revolution.) He responded that he would only correct an error in the understanding of the good minister, that Washington did not preside over any lodge nor had he visited

---

* The Illuminati was begun in 1776 (same year as the Declaration of Independence in America) by Johann Adam Weishaupt in Bavaria area of Europe (*Encyclopaedia Britannica*, Vol. XIV, 1911, 320); an anti-Christian, anti-civilization secret society of evil men who wanted to destroy existing cultural advancements and refinements by devious methods and deception (satanic influences). It eventually led to the tyranny in France (and elsewhere in Europe) of the French Revolution and its wicked tactics, as compared to the American system of Liberty under Christ.

a lodge more than once or twice in thirty years. Washington further observed that he did not believe that the American lodges would become contaminated with the evil influence of the Illuminati. In a second letter to Rev. Snyder (October 24, 1798), Washington further explains that he did not question that the doctrines of the Illuminati and Jacobinism had infected the United States. He says that he rather meant merely to say, "I did not believe that the lodges of freemasons in this country had, as societies, endeavored to propagate the diabolical tenets of the former, or pernicious principles of the latter, if they are susceptible of separation."* In other words, Washington believed that his American brethren possessed sufficient character not to succumb to the evil occult of the Illuminati, which parallels the beliefs of the ancient pagan power religions – the worship of the Baals.** Unfortunately, he over-estimated the wisdom of his American brothers, for not only has the Scottish Rite become the mainstream division of Masonry here, but America quickly lost its profound Biblical understanding of life in general, resulting in the deterioration of American Christian liberty that we know so painfully well today. Sorting out such details can give us a clearer picture of the historical reality and give us better ammunition for living for God more wisely.

Let us then enjoy the engaging story of Neil McKinlay as he seeks God *Through the Lattice*. As Paul the Apostle declares, "All things are lawful for me, but all things are not helpful; all things are lawful for me, but all things do not edify" (1 Corinthians 10:23, NKJV). Let us allow him to lead us, from his peculiar perspective, both to appreciate the good things we find in this life, and to discern and reject the things that do not edify so well.

Gerald Christian Nordskog
Publisher
Thanksgiving, November 25, 2010

---

* Jared Sparks, *The Writings of Washington* (Boston: American Stationers Company, 1837), Vol. XI, 314–315, 337.
**Rousas John Rushdoony, "The Meaning of Theocracy," www.theamericanview.com/index.php?id=668.

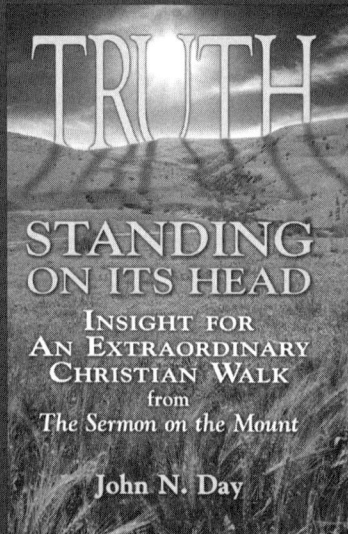

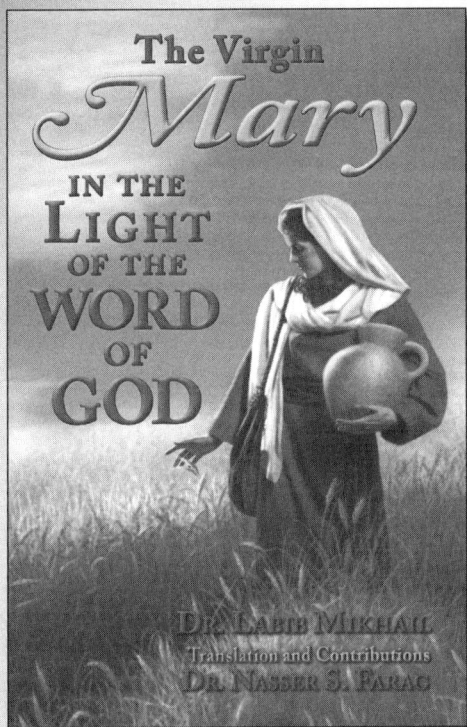

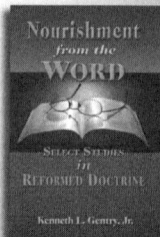

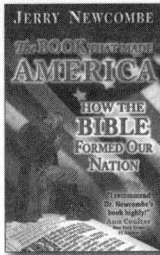

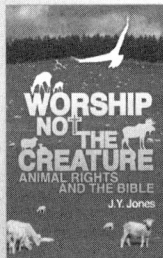